The Stage Race Handbook

A Comprehensive Guide on How to Train, prepare for and Complete Multi-Day Races Including: 4 Deserts Series and Marathon des Sables

Thomas Watson

Published internationally by Broadsea Press

Medical Disclaimer:
All information in this publication is the advice and recommendations of and personal to the author, and is not meant to replace that of a medical professional. Before partaking in any training or physical activity, the reader should consult with his or her medical professional.

THE STAGE RACE HANDBOOK

Special thanks to all the runners who have run with me over the years and informed the content of this book. Extra-big thanks to the following individuals who reviewed and contributed directly to the book you're now reading:

Tony Brammer
Rory Coleman (trademark used with kind permission)
Ainhoa Fernandez
Cynthia Fish
Brendan Funk
Peter Joergensen
Dean Karnazes
Dion Leonard
Lucja Leonard
Ash Mokhtari
Manu Pastor
Mark Roe
Filippo Rossi
Ryan Sandes
Sarah Sawyer

THE STAGE RACE HANDBOOK

TABLE OF CONTENTS

3

FOREWORD

Running is my passion. Not just running, but running far.

It wasn't always like this, though. There was a time when I was, like many people, caught up in a busy life. The busy trap. I had a great job, fancy car and was deep into the 'rat race'. On the night of my 30th birthday I realized this wasn't the life I had planned, so I ran 30 miles. That night forever changed the course of my life.

I began signing up for weekend races – before I knew it, my calendar was full, and I found myself traveling to ever more extreme and exotic places to run.

This is where stage races come in. They combine a lot of my favorite things – running, adventures and travelling to amazing places. When I completed the 4 Deserts Grand Slam back in 2008, those races took me to some of the wildest environments I've ever run in – whether it was the vast emptiness of the Atacama or living aboard a boat in Antarctica.

These races tap into that primordial feeling, which is the reason I run. They allow you to spend a long time out in the wild with nothing but your backpack and your running buddies. They have reminded me that there is magic in misery. When you're out in the desert, be it the Sahara or the Gobi, all you have is your own fortitude and willpower for company. What's not to love about that?

And the other thing about these races is the people you meet. They're not always what you'd expect. I've seen grandmothers and college professors, war veterans and people who have never run farther than a half marathon all line up at the start line of stage races. And they make it through. They survive and endure and their stories are some of the most inspiring I have ever heard.

I hope that this book serves to inspire you to push yourself, test the impossible and persevere. May you run far!

- **Dean Karnazes**
4 Deserts Champion & TIME '100 Most Influential People'
www.ultramarathonman.com

PREFACE

When I lined up at the start line of my first 250 km stage race, I had the wrong shoes, a backpack that chafed and was filled with the wrong types of food - which I struggled to eat over the next six days. That was in Madagascar, in September 2014. Six days of discomfort later, I managed to get myself over the finish line – and immediately began to take notes of what had worked and what hadn't.

Despite months of preparation and testing out equipment prior to that first event, I realised there were still several big gaps in my approach and knowledge of the most appropriate gear and strategies for stage races. During that race (and the four other stage races I have participated in since) I began speaking to other runners, both the novices and the veterans, to extract their preparation and training advice, strategies and gear recommendations.

After each subsequent race I made notes, solicited feedback and refined my approach. I've learned that while there's no 'one size fits all' approach to stage race preparation, training and running, there's a lot of solid steps you can follow from those who have gone before. That's what this book is – it's my distilled collection of notes, recommendations and advice. As testament to the information and strategies inside this book, I went from being a 'middle of the pack' runner (I came 100ᵗʰ out of 230 runners in that first Madagascar race) to getting two stage race podium places within two years – I came 3ʳᵈ out of 220 runners in the 4 Deserts Namibia race, only 20 months after that first race in Madagascar.

That isn't to say this book is aimed at making you *win* a stage race. The intention is to give you the advice and information you need to make the stage race as achievable as possible – to get you to finish comfortably, and maximise your enjoyment of the stage race. After all, something like a chafing backpack or the wrong food choices can have an immense impact on your experience of a week-long event.

So this book is really written for me – it's the book I wish I had back in early 2014, when I was preparing for that first event in Madagascar.
And keep an eye on marathonhandbook.com – I like to share as much advice and race reports as possible. If you want to get involved and write about a race you've done, or an aspect of stage racing you feel compelled to write about, let me know.

Enjoy, run far, and email me with any questions – I'll do my best to help you out.

- Thomas Watson, Marathon Handbook
hi@marathonhandbook.com

Runner Profiles
I've reached out to some of the stage racers I respect the most or feel have a compelling story to tell, and have included 'Runner Profiles' with interviews and tips from them between each chapter. They include some of the most decorated and experienced stage race runners, as well as one of the most experienced race volunteers in the game. Their insights hopefully provide some colour and depth that you'll find interesting.

Here's what to expect in the chapters which follow:

-        **An Introduction to Stage Races.** What is a stage race, how do they differ from other races, what different elements may be involved? What are some of the most popular formats and races? What's the difference between self-supported and supported? Why do people do stage races, and what type of people actually sign up for them.

-        **Researching Your Race.** This is the first step in stage race preparation.   There are several important areas of information you should research early on in your planning, in order to guide your training and gear purchases.   These include: environmental conditions, course features, levels of support, race format.

-        **Training.** Training for a stage race is a huge subject, with no 'one size fits all' approach.   In this section, I'll focus on what the typical training regimes are, which areas of training are important – and which are not.   I look at the various building blocks that should make up your training plan, and give my own training plan as an example. But this section is more guidance than prescriptive.   If you asked the 100 runners about their stage race preparation, you'll get 100 different answers.   I share the best and most proven training methods.

-        **Gear and Equipment.**   In this section I break down every item you might want to take with you on a stage race, from shoes to sanitary wipes, both mandatory and optional items. For the most part, I have discussed what your selection criteria   should   be,   rather   than   just   give   explicit recommendations.   I have broken things down for both self-supported and supported races. Also included are two example equipment spreadsheets, as well as guidance notes.   Keeping your pack as light as possible is important during a self-supported race, and should be considered for every piece of gear you intend to take. Here, I'll show you techniques to ensure your pack is practical and light (no pack needs to be over 10kg).

- **Nutrition and Hydration.** Food is your source of energy, so it's critical to find types of food that deliver that energy to you effectively, while being practical for your race. In this section I explore the various options for what to eat in a stage race, and look at what to eat before each stage, while running, and after you finish running each day. Hydration is another area you need to be aware of – how much you need to drink, why it's important to replenish your salts – and the best ways to do all this.

- **Preparation.** There's a lot more to stage race preparation than simply doing training and ordering all your gear online. Here, I explore many of the practical aspects of preparation you should consider – this can include a lot of logistical planning (especially if your race is in an exotic location), as well as testing your gear. There's a degree of mental preparation too – this means preparing for various scenarios, and knowing how to deal with unexpected setbacks such as blisters or other injuries.

- **The Stage Race.** Finally, it's here. In this section, I look at what things will be like during the actual race. After all your preparation, what you should actually expect and prepare for. I've included several tips on how to cope and strategise when things get tough. This section essentially walks you through each stage of the race.

- **Conclusion.** Here I've pulled everything together - a quick re-cap of the key points that you will want to take away from this book.

1. An Introduction to Stage Races

What is a Stage Race?

A stage race, for the sake of this book, is a foot race that takes place over more than one day - or stage. They typically cover between two and six stages.

Given there are so many stage races with different formats and elements, it's a wide field to try and categorise. Stage races are sometimes referred to as **multi-stage races** - it's the same thing.

Here are some typical features of a stage race, though remember that every event is different:

- Typical distance is an average of 30-50km / day
- Spread over 2-6 stages, or days
- Often features one longer day, of 70-100km
- Runners sleep in tents or other provided accommodation each night
- There are checkpoints roughly every 10 km, typically with water
- May be self-supported (runners carry all food and equipment with them), supported (runners only carry a few small pieces of equipment, food is provided) or somewhere in between
- Usually stage races are held in areas of special interest - exotic countries, challenging environments and remote locales.

Of course, not every stage race follows the above rules. There are many great two and three-day stage races, and at the other end of the spectrum there are stage races which stretch on for 10 days or more.

The information in this book is primarily aimed at the most popular type of stage race - five or six stages, roughly 150 miles / 250 km in total, self-supported events. However, it should also be applicable for shorter and longer events, as well as supported events.

Stage Races - Why Are They Different?

Stage races are wildly different to normal foot races, both in how you approach them and what you will experience.

In a normal, one-day event - be it a 10km, marathon or 100km - your goal is normally to get to the finish line in the quickest time you can. It's one block of sustained effort, with a clear end point. Whatever happens, it's going to be over in just a few hours - then you can sit back, relax and recover. Even injuries are secondary during a one-day event - if you start to feel that old knee pain creep up, you can choose to push through it and worry about it later.

Stage races are fundamentally different. In stage races, you have to keep yourself moving forward day after day. This means that going as fast as you can is not a sustainable strategy, and will likely get you in trouble early on. You've got to constantly be conservative - hold something back for the next day, or next few days.

You also have to become a master strategist - if you have to carry all your food for an entire week on your back, how do you decide how much you're going to take, and when you're going to eat it? Carrying a 70g Clif bar in your pack for five days - or 200km, let's say - adds up to a lot of energy used (perhaps more than the Clif bar provides?).

The magnitude of the undertaking in a stage race means that many runners simply have the goal of finishing, and any element of competition is secondary to the physical challenge and the cross-country journey they go through.

The goal of this book is to prepare you to the best degree possible - to give you the strategies and tactics to have the most comfortable and enjoyable stage race experience you can have.

Types of Stage Race Explained

I briefly covered the different types of stage race above, now I'll give a little more detail.

Self-supported Stage Races

Self-supported stage races mean you take everything you need for that week with you on your back - this means all your food, clothing and equipment. Water is provided by the organisers, as well as (usually) some form of tents or accommodation. A self-supported race is a huge undertaking and requires a significant amount of planning, testing and training in order to complete it comfortably.

Self-supported races can be physically and mentally challenging - you have to carry all your equipment while you run, and in the campsites you have to be entirely self-sufficient. A typical pack will weigh around 10kg at the start of a 6-stage event, and around 6kg by the end when you have eaten all your food.

Examples of self-supported stage races include Marathon des Sables and the 4 Deserts series.

Supported Stage Races

A **'supported'** stage race is one in which many of your needs are provided by the organizers. They will typically transport your 'drop bag' from campsite to campsite, leaving you to only carry the essentials in a small pack as you run. Meals may be provided, or there may be restaurants near each campsite. Alternatively, you may have to bring your own meals in your drop bag and look after yourself. The level of support and comfort can vary, from staying in basic tents to staying in 4-star hotels.

Examples of supported stage races include the Burgos 'The Way Of Legends' race in Northern Spain (an example of a boutique stage race), and the Global Limits race series.

Other formats

Many stage races fall somewhere between self-supported and supported - the important thing is to properly research and understand what each stage race provides and what it expects of you. I cover these topics in-depth in the next chapter, Researching Your Race.

Who Runs Stage Races?

Stage races attract an interesting mix of people, and not all are long-term serious runners. In fact, those 'competitive' types tend to be in the minority in most stage races. What you'll find instead is a broad mix of people from many walks of life. If marathons and ultras attract the 'type A' personalities, stage races attract the more adventurous.

Marathon des Sables has more working professionals chasing a physical and mental *journey* than semi-pro runners competing for the top 50. The 4 Deserts race series attracts more retirees, business people and others seeking a unique experience, than hard-core runners.

Many of the semi-pro runners shy away from stage races anyway. A week-long event takes a lot of time to train for, and carries a relatively high-risk of injury - at least for those who are going as fast as they can. There isn't normally a big competitive field in stage races, and none of them (with the possible exception of the Marathon des Sables) is big enough for the podium finishers to attract serious PR - at least compared to single-day events.

For many, the people you meet during stage races is the best part of the week. The shared experience of covering long distances by foot and sharing food and tents each evening brings people together. Plus, stage races tend to attract interesting people.

"Ultimately, the people I meet during the race are the highlights of the race. The runners and the volunteers make the whole experience completely unforgettable. Some of my best friends are the people I have met in these races and incredibly after just a couple of days of sharing a tent or a few hours – not even, more like minutes – of conversation on the run or around the campfire have created long-lasting, close friendships."

- **Ash Mokhtari, serial stage race runner**

Marathon des Sables attracts runners from 17 to 78 years old. The average age of a 4 Deserts runner is 38, and there is typically around an 80/20 male/female split.

Stage races also vary wildly in size - Marathon des Sables, the largest, attracts 1200+ runners each year. The 4 Deserts race series typically have 200-300 runners per race, while there exists dozens of smaller races that typically keep their head count well below 100 racers. As you may expect, the smaller races tend to have a strong spirit of camaraderie - you are likely to chat to every other runner, as opposed to the bigger races. That's not to say camaraderie doesn't exist in the larger races, quite the opposite - but the sheer number of runners may mean you are often surrounded by strangers.

The Mentality of a Stage Race = Grit

Stage races are a different breed of race, and require a different set of characteristics to complete than simply physical fitness. It's not uncommon to see an experienced runner drop out after the first or second day of a stage race, while the 60-year-old grandmother with no prior running experience will continue to trot happily to the end. The physical fitness level required to complete a stage race is very different to that required to run a marathon, as we'll see.

Stage races can be a real test of your mental mettle. Developing a knee injury during a marathon is tough, but if you develop one on the first day of a six-day stage race, you are going to have a pretty tough week ahead of you. Many stage race competitors suffer such ailments - be it injury, fatigue, illness or shoe/equipment issues - that make each step of their race a real measure of willpower. The difference between those that choose to continue and those who decide to stop is often their willpower, or grit.

Much has been written about this measure of perseverance, and how it can correlate to success in various fields of life. Perhaps this, more than anything, is why you find such a variety of interesting and adventurous people at stage races - they all have a measure of grit inside them, and that's what has attracted them to the event.

Finding a Stage Race

Now I have introduced what a stage race is, you hopefully have an overview of what to expect. If you are looking for a stage race, as well as the aforementioned Marathon des Sables and 4 Deserts race series, I can recommend heading over to www.stageraces.com for a comprehensive database of stage races around the world.

Let's Talk About Walking

Despite stage races being considered a 'running event', the truth is that most of us walk a significant portion of them. Even the front-runners will occasionally stop charging ahead and slow down to a brisk stride at times. In fact, there's a large chunk of the participants of every stage race that walk the whole thing.

Obviously walking 250km takes a little longer than running it, but you'll typically find that the walkers are calmer, more upbeat and handle the stress of the stage race well - and probably have a higher rate of completing the races.

The advice in this book is aimed at all stage race participants, but if you are planning to walk the majority of your stage race there are some specific tips that can help you prepare better. Rather than scatter them throughout the advice sections which follow, I thought I'd collect them here. Special thanks for contributions from **Cynthia Fish**, who has walked more races than Scott Jurek has run (probably).

Training

Walkers should train with their fully-loaded pack more than runners should. Walkers are essentially hikers, and while hiking with a pack will tire you out, it doesn't screw up your form like running with a pack will.

Walkers are also going to have a tougher time during the race. They spend more time walking than sleeping, and will usually arrive at each day's camp hours after the runners have finished, eaten, cleaned up and rested. They also often arrive back to camp in the dark, and have to tend to blisters, eat and clean themselves up all while not tripping over their snoozing tent mates.

For these reasons, walkers should try and develop a certain psychological fortitude as much as possible.

Walkers get much greater benefit from the use of walking poles, too. They help take the load off when forging ahead, and often groups of walkers will share poles, rotating them throughout the day.

"We - the walkers - should practice being miserable... going out in the rain, in the snow in the cold, in the dark. We have to learn how to manage nasty conditions ... no quick run home for us.

Cross training is especially important, and so is mountain hiking, bicycling, etc. If you bring along slower family friends, load up your pack with everyone's lunches and water.

We take up to four to five hours longer over the day. Generally, we carry heavier bags. The happy ones carry and use sticks. In many cases we come in after dark, and we rest/recover and dine quite quickly. We tend to be a cheerful lot, lots of jokes and mutual support. We "race" against the cutoffs and the sweepers and we look anxiously over our shoulder to check for the camel. We really are about just finishing...

The back of the pack group, the ones who are surprised about how long it takes to cover 42 kms a day, or the ones who have been laid low by an injury are a different breed, but the turtles are nothing if not welcoming. Turtles have trained for the walking, and back of the packer are those who didn't expect to be there. Nevertheless, we persist. "

- **Cynthia Fish, certified walker and member of the 4 Deserts Grand Slam Plus club (there are only eight members in the world).**

23

RACER PROFILE: SARAH SAWYER

Sarah Sawyer makes no secret of the fact that she loves multi-day races, primarily because they combine two of her favourite pastimes - running and travel. She has completed a number of multi-day races around the world, including Racing the Planet 250k Patagonia (1st female), Racing the Planet 250k Ecuador (1st female) and 4 Deserts Atacama Crossing (2nd female).

Basically, if there's a multi-day race in a location she wants to visit on holiday, then she's on the start line! When she's not running multi-day races she runs everything from 5ks to 100 mile ultramarathons in the mountains, on trails, on the track and on road.

For more of her personal running blog, visit shetravelssheruns.wordpress.com

For running coaching and Pilates teaching, check out: www.pilatesandrunningwithsarah.com

What was it about stage races that first appealed to you?

I'm embarrassed to say it was watching James Cracknell's 'Toughest Race on Earth' MdS DVD that initially seeded the idea of multi-day racing to me. I'd completed a few marathons and was just starting to dabble in ultras, and to a very amateur inexperienced runner, the idea of running the equivalent of 4 x marathons and 1 x ultramarathon in a week seemed almost impossible to me, however the seed was planted and before I knew it I was googling 'multi-day desert races'.

I initially opted for the 4 Deserts Sahara Race (which was based in Jordan the year I ran it) as I'd always wanted to visit Jordan and this race started at Wadi Rum and you ran to Petra, which was going to be some finish line! A number of people remarked that there were easier ways to see Petra (ie walk there from your hotel!), however I can't imagine there are more satisfying ways to see Petra, knowing you've travelled 155 miles on foot to get there!

I had nearly 2 years from initially booking the race to the race starting, so I had a lot of time to get used to the idea and prepare. In an era of materialism (of which I'm guilty of as much as anyone – I know I don't need 24 pairs of trainers!), I loved the idea of going back to basics for a week and surviving with just what I could carry on my back.

Also, I openly admit to being the most organised person in the world so I loved the planning and organising and all the lists that I got to make, that is required pre-race before you even get to the start line!

How has your preparation for stage races evolved?

I think the biggest difference in my preparation has been that I've gone from the mindset of being 'completer' to 'competer'. For my first multi-day race my starting rucksack weight was

9kg, this dropped to 8kg for Ecuador, just over 7kg for Atacama and then to an all-time low of 6.9kg for Patagonia (and this was despite there being several more items of mandatory kit for Patagonia).

For my first multi-day race, my only goal was 'completion' so although I was mindful of my rucksack not weighing too much, I certainly wasn't obsessive about the weight of it, so I took way more calories than I needed to, and I even took a change of top for camp (although I quickly realised by camp 2 that this was a pointless item and it was binned!).

As I got more experience of multi-day racing, I learnt exactly how many calories I need a day to be able to run well. I also use the bulk of my mandatory calorie allowance on days 1-5 and just go hungry on the rest day, as the vast majority of the running has been done by then. I remember on my first race in Jordan waking up on the rest day and having two 800 calorie freeze-dried meals to eat, the last thing I wanted or needed!

I also sought out the lightest kit where I could, so for example for Patagonia my headtorch and back-up headtorch in Patagonia had a combined weight of just 33g and my waterproof trousers which were mandatory kit weighed in at 79g. I learnt that with every item of mandatory or optional kit there are ways to shave a few vital grams off it if you shop around or improvise, which will bring your total rucksack weight down. I also try and multi-purpose items where I can. So for example, I'm a huge fan of Mountain Fuel energy drinks which combine part of my daily calorie allowance alongside my mandatory electrolyte requirements.

My training has also got a lot smarter. For Jordan I just did lots of long runs along Brighton seafront with my rucksack – hardly ideal preparation for a race in the desert! For subsequent races, I've tried to make sure the terrain I'm training on is more like what I'm going to be racing on, so virtually all my runs are off-road, and when I can I get to more technical terrain such as in the Brecon Beacons. Also, I still incorporate speedwork in my training; if you want to race multi-day races with the view to hopefully being towards the top of the field, then you do need that speed as days 1 – 4 always tend to be shorter than marathon distance.

How does Pilates compliment your ultra-running?

I'm a huge advocate of Pilates and yoga to compliment my running. I truly believe that without it, I wouldn't be able to run the distances I do in training and racing, and stay injury-free. Pilates has been so useful for strength, conditioning and for a strong core for carrying the rucksack. I use yoga to improve my flexibility and also use hot yoga if I'm going to be racing in a hot climate.

Is it hard to find time to train sufficiently for stage races?

The hardest thing for me for stage races is not the time you need to train for a multi-day race, but training with your pack. Your runs are slower, the pack affects your running form, and at the end of the day it's not natural to be running with a 7+kg load on your back!

Because I have quite a strong endurance background, I already have that as my base, and then will just train with the pack for about 6 weeks before the race. I find 6 weeks is the optimum length of time for me to get used to running with the full pack, yet it's not too long that it puts too much stresses on my body.

I think there's a misconception that you need to run really high mileage in training for a multi-day race. I tend to peak at around 70-80 miles a week and it's more about the quality of those miles, rather than just churning out lots and lots of long, slow miles.

What advice would you give to someone preparing for their first ever stage race?

Don't sacrifice on sleep and calories. So, invest in a good quality sleeping bag that withstands temperatures to colder that you're likely to get and don't even think about saving weight on a sleeping mat – every race I've done I see someone try this and it always ends in tears (and sleepless night sleeps!).

Similarly, with calories, races will stipulate the minimum amount of calories you need, but find out how many you need to race well everyday. You're going to be in a calorie deficit, but it's making sure you don't cross that line and it impacts your performance, so whatever you do make sure you have enough calories.

Any 'secret sauce' tips/quirky things you do to help you during stage races?

Sleep! Never underestimate the 'power' of sleep. I'm always in my sleeping bag for 7pm in multi-day races and normally sleep through to 5am. I know that if I have enough sleep then I can get up and run well every day.

2. RESEARCHING YOUR RACE

Doing some research on your stage race is one of the first steps you should take during your preparation. The climate, course conditions and level of support will all influence how your race goes, and you need to prepare accordingly.

In this chapter I explore each variable you need to research and consider, and how it might influence your preparation. The information you need should all be online - either on the race organiser's website or through a quick Google search. If you aren't having much joy, you can always drop the organisers an email.

Nowadays, most race organisations have an active social media community which can be a fantastic resource for asking questions and getting to know other runners. Facebook groups are very common and are a great way to connect directly with the organisers and other runners.

Climate

The climate of your race locale will really dictate what kind of experience you are going to have. The main areas to look at are - rain and weather, temperature, humidity, and altitude.

Rain and Weather

Weather is an important race factor that you should research now, if you haven't already.

What are the chances of rain in your race location? Will it be windy? Are tropical storms a threat? A good place to look are reports and photos from previous events, if they are available.

The risk of wet weather informs a lot of your equipment choices – as a minimum, you need to have waterproofing to protect your torso and your backpack from the elements, and any other mandatory equipment the race organiser specifies. There are many ultra-lightweight jackets that are specifically designed for running, and some have additional volume to cover your backpack too. You should consider taking additional waterproof bags (zip-locks and black refuse bags can be used) in order to protect equipment from the rain and segregate wet gear.

During multi-stage events with the risk of rain, you should prepare yourself mentally for the possibility of having to wake up and put on wet gear, and start running. In these conditions, using lubricant is even more important - running in wet clothing is a recipe for severe chafing and blisters.

The race organiser may have specific equipment requirements if rain is likely.

Depending on your race location, sand storms are entirely possible too. If so, have something at hand to use as a mask -

a neckscarf that you can also wrap around your head to protect your ears is a good idea.

Temperature

A quick Google search can tell you the temperature at the race location specific to that time of year – it's worth looking at the highs, lows and the average.

Running in high temperatures can be challenging, and it's common for runners coming from cooler Western countries to suffer from heat exhaustion. Unfortunately, preparing yourself for temperatures of 40°C + when you live in the cooler parts of the northern hemisphere is not easy.
Runners use different (and novel) techniques for preparing for the heat.

Using a sauna is probably the most accessible way for most of us to simulate high temperatures, and although you can't run in one you can use one after your daily workout. Doing this for a few weeks prior to your race will help your body build up more tolerance to heat.

Another heat-acclimatization option is to take up bikram yoga (yoga in a hot, steamy room). Another popular technique is to run with additional layers on, building up an uncomfortable heat and getting used to pushing through that feeling of cloying sweat.

Remember to consider the night-time temperature too, as this will influence your choice of sleeping bag if you are camping, and how many layers to bring. The race organizer should be able to advise you on this. Desert climates can be scorchingly hot through the day, but shiveringly cold at night - and many runners underestimate the latter.

Humidity

Many people swear they can handle the heat, but the humidity kills them. Running through the 40°C Amazon rainforest with 93% humidity is a completely different challenge to running through the desert at 40°C (typical 25% humidity).

Humidity affects your respiratory system faster than heat alone, and on a humid day with no breeze your sweat can't evaporate or blow away – effectively coating you in a warm, slick layer of insulation. This means your body temperature will shoot up. In these instances, the best thing you can do is to slow down and control your exertion levels, take regular breaks, drink water and seek shade where possible.

To prepare yourself, using saunas or practicing bikram yoga are the two most effective methods of simulating hot humidity in cold-weather countries.

Altitude

Running at altitude comes with its own set of rules. Altitude affects runners in different ways - shortness of breath is common, and dizziness or nausea are possible. Older runners tend to be affected more easily than younger ones.

The **most common approach** to running a race at altitude is simply **to arrive at the race location 2-3 days before the start of the race**, to allow your body to adjust to the altitude. During the race, you can expect to feel more tired and out-of-breath than usual. Simply factor this in, and don't over-exert or try and match your sea-level degree of exertion.

There are a few ways you can simulate, or prepare for running at altitude if you live in a low-lying area.

The **best, and most practical way to simulate altitude while training is to find a gym with a hypoxic chamber** – these are sealed rooms where the oxygen content is lowered to simulate altitude. They typically have a few treadmills, exercise bikes and light weights in them – hopefully there is one near you.

Some runners have tried training with an 'elevation mask', or 'resistance mask'. These restrict the flow of air into your mouth, making it harder to breathe. While this effect is similar to the feeling you may experience at altitude, the truth is that breathing at altitude is harder because there is less oxygen in the air, not because you're breathing through a restriction. So while these masks definitely provide some form of resistance training and lung strengthening, the science says it is not an accurate simulation of breathing at altitude.

It is possible to invest in an 'altitude tent', usually used by hardcore mountain climbers – this is a sealed tent you put around your bed with a device that lowers the oxygen content in the air, so as you sleep your body gets acclimatized to the altitude conditions. However, these usually cost up to five figures(!) if you can't hire one.

Course Conditions

Gradients (hills)

Running hills is a completely different skill to running on the flat. Running uphill is hard if you're just used to flat surfaces, and running downhill puts extreme loads on your joints.

If your race has hills, you should look to incorporate some into your run training.

The typical advice for running downhill is to shorten your stride and keep your knees bent! The key to this is practice of course. It has been shown that running downhill increases eccentric loading on the legs which can lead to a higher rate of injury. While you don't want to be practicing yourself into an injury, not being prepared for the loading of running downhill can lead to injury during the stage race.

Underfoot Terrain

Dirt tracks? Tarmac? Sharp stones? Snow? Whatever the terrain is, you should train in a similar environment as much as is feasible, to prepare yourself. This way, you can get used to the terrain and test out your running shoes. Remember that soft sand and snow both sap a lot of energy per step. If there's a lot of sand, or loose snow, then this is going to make your race much harder - your walking/running style changes, and uses a lot more energy. You can train specifically for sand/snow by jumping rope, doing step-up exercises - or actually training in sand. In these cases, a set of gaiters should be seriously considered (this is discussed in the gear section later).

Water Crossings

The organisers will typically warn you if water crossings are expected, but may not detail exactly where they will be, or how many to expect. Runners approach water crossings differently – some plough through and keep going with wet feet, while others remove their socks and shoes and wade across.

Wet feet, clamped in wet socks and shoes, can potentially end your race (see the chapter on foot maceration later). If your feet are already blistered or torn up, the damp conditions will just exacerbate the problem. Therefore, if in doubt, we recommend packing a spare pair of socks if you are anticipating a water crossing.

Race Details

The specifics decided by the organiser have a big impact on your race. Make sure you familiarise yourself early on with the route map and itinerary, as well as the daily mileage.

Race Rules

Familiarise yourself with the rules of the race, paying attention to things like:

- Cut-off times
- Water allowances
- Time penalties and what they are for
- Bib and patch requirements.

Level of Support

It's worth doing a bit of research to find out just how well supported a race is before you set off. Marathon des Sables, for example, has an army of infrastructure shipped to the desert for the week of their race. Between the helicopters, dozens of doctors and other volunteers, you certainly get the sense that you'd be in good hands if something went wrong.

The 4 Deserts race series typically has a doctor at each checkpoint, and often a 'roving doctor' in a vehicle following the race.

Smaller races will typically have less support infrastructure - but that's not to say they don't have the same level of professionalism as the bigger races.

Course and Mileage

Ensure you are familiar with how the course is going to be marked. It's pretty standard for the course director to use markers such as tape and spray paint to mark the route, which is pretty easy to follow. Some races may issue GPS devices with the route pre-programmed into them for you to follow, and others may have minimal marking but involve some kind of orienteering.

Ensure you're aware how the course will be marked and that you bring along any necessary equipment that the organiser advises on. Depending on the level of support, it can often be valuable to stick with other runners while out on the trails, to support each other.

What's Provided?

Find out what is provided by the race organisers. As a minimum, you'll get water. Most races, such as the 4 Deserts series, also provide hot water at the campsites. Find out a little about where you are going to sleep - most races provide tents, and nothing else. This means that if you want a sleeping mat, you will have to carry it yourself.

What's on the Mandatory Equipment List?

This is an important one - find out what is mandatory for you to carry with you. Supported races may have two mandatory equipment lists - a list of items you need to carry with you during the race, and a list of items that you just need in your drop bag. Equipment is discussed in detail later on.

Checkpoints

Find out the frequency of the checkpoints and what's going to be available at them, so you can plan accordingly. Most long races have a checkpoint around every 10km, and the minimum you'd expect at them is a water supply and a volunteer. Better-equipped checkpoints may have electrolyte drinks, food and medical support.

Sleeping conditions

Sleeping conditions vary from race to race, and it's worth finding out as much as you can before leaving home. Are you going to be in tents – and if so, how many people per tent? If you're in homestays or public buildings, is mosquito netting required, or provided?

No matter how tired you are, the sounds of other runners milling around, or wild animals out on the prowl, can keep you awake. Consider taking a pair of throwaway ear buds (like the ones they give you on a plane) and a face mask. Some runners take airplane neck pillows with them.

If you bring a pad, be sure to test it out (actually sleep on it!) before the race. They can take some getting used to, so it is worth testing them out in order to familiarise yourself with how they'll feel. Some pads crinkle all night with every small movement. If you move in your sleep a lot, this can be a major annoyance.

RACER PROFILE: RORY COLEMAN

Rory Coleman is a marathon phenomenon. He began his distance running career in 1994 and hasn't looked back - having now run over 1000 marathons, including 245 ultras, he is also the UK's leading ultra-marathon coach.

Rory is no stranger to stage races either, having run the Marathon des Sables 14 times - more than any other British competitor as well as the 4 Deserts Atacama Crossing.

His coaching and #average2awesome training are helping runners all over the UK achieve their goals.

His website: www.colemancoaching.co.uk

What was it about Marathon des Sables that first appealed to you?

I'd seen double amputee Chris Moon MBE featured on TV running the Marathon des Sables in 1997 and made plans for it to feature whilst trying to run 100 marathons in 1999. At that time, running a six-day, six-stage race was unheard of in the UK and I was looking for a race that could stretch my limits of human endurance.

How has your preparation for MdS evolved?

For my first MdS, I bought the equipment I needed, rucksack, sleeping bag etc. at my local Outdoor Store, as well as some rather heavy self-heating meals. My MdS training was a basic marathon training programme that you'd use to run a big city marathon. My rucksack nowadays is full of super-light gear and chosen for its suitability from a spectrum of ultra-marathon running specialists weighing-in at no more than 6.5kgs including all my food. Sand-Gaiters hadn't been invented when I first raced but now there are some great breathable ones with Velcro that don't let in a grain of sand, which enables me to be blister-free.

How does MdS influence other aspects of your life, whether personal or professional?

My first MdS turned my life upside down and changed me for the better I believe. During the race, I realised that my career and my private-life both needed an update. I've been very fortunate to make my passion my career and met my wife Jenny at the MdS - finding someone that shares my passion for desert-running as much as I do was ultra-special in 2009. I now train over 100 MdS hopefuls a year and pass on all my MdS knowledge to them.

Is it hard to find the time to train sufficiently for races like Marathon des Sables?

There's always time to train, especially if it's something you enjoy doing and know will pay off in the race. I think of it as an investment plan or savings account where by stacking in at least an hour a day of exercise can be withdrawn during the race itself. Training starts the moment you press enter on the race-website and as coming home without the medal isn't an option, it's always good to have a 12-week plan written for you to keep you on track.

What advice would do you give to someone preparing for their first ever MdS?

I underline that the race is a 'Self-Sufficiency Race' not a marathon or ultra-marathon and can be as easy or as hard as folk it. My three very simple rules are, Don't weigh much. Don't take much and Do some training. Being lean and light makes a massive time-difference in being boiled out in the midday sun or relaxing in the shelter of a tent. Learning the pace that's quick enough to get you out of the sun but not to break you is the key - it's always a lot slower than folk think and equates to whatever's run in MPH in the UK being transferred into KPH in Morocco.

Any 'secret sauce' tips / quirky things you do to help you during your MdS?

I love the support of my tent-mates and the banter but I really enjoy the solitude of the desert and I exclude the other 1000+ runners from my world by listening to music for the whole race. I find that way I can exclude any distractions from my running rhythm and any 'energy vampires' that might project their negativity onto me. I always remind myself at the start-line each day that I've chosen to do the MdS and how lucky I am to be able to take part in 'The world's toughest footrace'.

Share a particularly memorable or favourite race experience.

To be asked to train and run the MdS with Sir Ranulph Fiennes must be the pinnacle of my MdS experiences. Sir Ranulph is one of my all-time 'Boy's Own Heroes' and I was extremely privileged to be part of his world leading up to and during the 2015 race. Hearing his amazing stories one-to-one in the dark of the long stage will stay with me forever. As for which MdS, it must be the 'Wet year' of 2009, as it was a real stand-out year raining so hard the race was cut to four stages but made longer and tougher to keep 'The world's toughest footrace' super-tough. It was my highest position finish and the one I'm most proud of.

What keeps you motivated to keep returning to MdS?

Every April, the MdS offers an opportunity to take a 'time-out'. Time-out to think about the previous life. Time to reflect and make plans for the next 12 months, without distraction. The race strips everyone bare and I find the days in the desert are re-energising and it never fails to make me realise the importance of our families and children are and how unimportant possessions and money are. I know that my recovery from Guillain-Barré Syndrome in 2016 was much improved by having the MdS in 2017 as a fitness goal. Months on from completing the race, most folk me included, get some very 'Rose-Tinted Specs' about the whole MdS Experience and want to relive their desert experience and once the MdS is your blood it's there for life.

3. TRAINING

Training for a stage race is a huge subject, with no 'one size fits all' approach. In this section, I'll focus on what the typical training regimes are, which areas of training are common to most runners and proven to be effective.

I look at the various building blocks that should make up your training plan, and give my example training plan. But remember – this section is more guidance than prescriptive. If you asked 100 runners about their stage race preparation, you'd get 100 different answers. Everyone has different backgrounds and ability levels, and everyone has different expectations of what it means to be 'race ready'. I'll focus on the areas I feel are important to get your body ready to cover serious distance, day after day, while minimising discomfort.

Many stage race runners neglect cross-training, or any kind of strength-training. To me, this is a mistake - I can only speak from my own experience, but I've found that following a strength training programme really helped my endurance in the latter few stages of my stage races. I cover this a little more in the Cross Training section later.

Run Training

There should be various elements to your run training, in order for you to strengthen your running base and build up your mileage.

Note for walkers: many people simply walk or march for the majority of a stage race. If this is your intention, great! You don't need to focus so hard on running during your training. However, you should still use some of the activities discussed below to build up your base hiking fitness - for example, you should get used to doing a long hike every week in order to build up your endurance, and do 'doubles' (two hikes on two consecutive days) so your body gets used to moving on worn-out legs.

What are the goals of my running training?
The goals of your running training should be:

- To build up a strong running endurance base that allows you to cross long distances with minimal issues or injuries.

- To build up a level of endurance that lets you get up and run day-after-day on a five or six stage event.

The amount of run training you need will depend on what your base fitness level is, and what level you want to be at when you start the race.

A simple rule of thumb for a stage race is that prior to the race, you should have at least completed:

- A long continuous run of 60-70km (say 80% of the longest stage of your race)

- Two back-to-back marathons on consecutive days.

44

"My rule of thumb for any stage racer is that if you wanna finish in the top 25% of the competition, you gotta run 1/4th of the total distance every week for at least 6 months and that's with a race weight backpack. So to finish in the top 25% you gotta run 60-65 km/week with a backpack."
- **Ash Mokhtari, serial stage race runner**

Now let's look at some of the building blocks of a good stage race training plan:

Weekly Long Runs

Very long, slow runs are a staple of every good distance runner's training programme. I normally do these on weekend mornings when I have plenty of time. They help you gradually increase your maximum mileage. Pace during these long runs is not important, unless you're training to compete. I gradually increase the mileage until one month before my event, when you should peak - at say 60km.

Doubles

Performing two long runs on consecutive days. Again, these are important training for stage races – you want to get used to waking up and running on tired legs. Do these over Saturdays / Sundays in the months leading up to your race (I normally tie these in with the long run - I'll do the long run on a Saturday and a shorter run on the Sunday, in order to get my legs used to running when they've been used the previous day).

Typical Run

Your typical 10km training run, at a comfortable pace is a great training tool – you can bash it out a couple of times per week, in the morning or after work – without having to think or apply yourself too much. These complement your weekend long runs very well, by keeping your legs active and topping up your training mileage.

Interval Training

Interval training, and tempo runs, means running at varying degrees of intensity, and is a much more dynamic way of working out than plodding along at a constant rate. These help your dynamic running and speed rather than your distance running capacity, so they're ones for those runners looking to compete. Dig out your GPS watch and do some pace drills.

Increasing Your Mileage

When you are starting out your stage race training, it's worth following the **10% Rule**. This is an old rule of thumb that says runners should only increase their mileage by 10% each week in training to avoid over-training injuries. While it may seem a little conservative, it helps ward off over-training and can give your training plan some structure.

A "recovery" week every 3-4 weeks where you aren't increasing by 10% is very beneficial, for example, Wk 1: 50km, Wk2: 55km, Wk3: 60km, Wk4: 60km.

Running with a Pack

If you are preparing for a self-supported stage race, you may be considering training with your pack. Having spoken to several ultra-runners and race doctors about this, the consensus seems to be that training with a 10kg pack too much will hamper your running form and increase your chance of injury. The upside of running with a pack is that you get used to knowing how it feels, you can try it out and make any adjustments to minimise chafing, and feel a bit more comfortable. It is important to at least be familiar with how it feels to run with a pack, as it changes your running style a lot!

Therefore, during stage race preparation I typically run with my pack only once per week – usually just for a 10km. However, other runners train more heavily with their pack (see the interview with Ryan Sandes).

Tapering

In the final month before your stage race, you should slow down, train less, relax more – and arrive at the start line feeling fresh and ready to go. Many elite runners barely taper at all - just easing off in the final 3-4 days. What you've got to consider is the risk of injury if you don't taper - you want to avoid introducing new strain or injury in those final precious weeks. When you reach the start line, you'd rather have under-trained and be injury-free than have over-trained and given yourself an injury.

Injuries

They happen. You shouldn't run through pain if it persists during exercise. However, rather than let them stop you in your tracks, be proactive – get the problem diagnosed by a reputable physio and work on fixing it. Most injuries related to running shouldn't stop you from running as long as you are addressing it properly.

If, like many runners, you are struggling with "runner's knee" (www.painscience.com has a ton of free resources about treatment).

Cross Training

For runners, cross training means doing any type of exercise which compliments your running training. Almost any form of workout or exercise will complement your running fitness, though some are better than others. Here, I explore the different options runners have when it comes to cross training – and which ones will have a positive impact on your running game.

It's always surprising how few distance runners actually cross train – many just get up and run, maybe with a few minimal stretches. However, a proper cross training regime can not only strengthen the rest of your body, but can up your running game too. It makes you much less injury prone and will improve your performance.

When you're in training for an event, free time to train can be a luxury in-between everything else in life – and actual running will always be the most important form of training. It's a fact that some of us just don't have the time in our schedules for any form of cross training – but if you can squeeze in just an hour or two a week, the results will show themselves during your event. I personally have found that working out in the gym has had a significant impact on my endurance, which helps a lot when you're several hours into the long day of a stage race.

In his book 'Running Strong', Dr Jordan Metzl speaks a lot about the 'kinetic chain' – this is all the muscles, bones and joints that move when you go running. The problem is, running loads can create weaknesses and imbalances in these areas, which will end up leading to injuries. You can have the strongest calves in the world, but if you've got weak hamstrings or glutes then you're heading for a knee injury. So how to combat this?

Stretches for Runners

The easiest way to save yourself from these problems is basic stretches and strength training. Dedicating 10-20 minutes each morning to stretching and strengthening is a pretty solid way to reduce your chances of injury drastically.

Some stretches I find useful for running (you can type these into Youtube to find good videos on how to do them):

- Hamstring Stretch
- Calf Raises
- Kneeling Hip Flexor Stretch
- Standing Lunges
- Squats
- Arm / Shoulder stretches (especially important once you introduce the backpack)

Squats in particular build up functional strength throughout the legs, minimise muscular imbalances that lead to injury and help with range-of-motion.

Low Intensity Work-outs

Doing low-intensity activities are awesome for maintaining your fitness on non-running days and giving your upper body a workout too.

Swimming is great for recovery days, as it's low-impact on the entire body, while letting you stretch out and do some cardio. Yoga, pilates and other non-contact activities can help you focus on your muscles and flexibility.

Strength Training - Gym Work

To me, if you want to focus on being a stronger runner, your cross-training time should mainly be spent in the gym. I find that hitting the gym three times a week has had a huge impact on my long distance running performance (and specifically stage races). In particular, one of those gym days will be dedicated to only working on my legs. That's not to say that the upper body can be neglected – working on good upper body strength and a strong core means that you have better form and are much less injury-prone when you run long distances. A weak core, hips and glutes contribute to so many injuries, doing some gym work can help recalibrate some of those imbalances in your system.

I tend to focus on a lot of body-weight work to strengthen my core and relative strength – so things like push-ups, pull-ups, squats (once you are comfortable with body-weight squats, you can add dumbbells). From my own experience, I've found that since I've incorporated strength training into my workout, my endurance has gone through the roof. Many hours into ultramarathons, I still feel strong as I pass others who are bent-double and clearly in physical discomfort. It's the main area I feel most distance runners neglect, and I always try and persuade my running friends to spend more time at the gym.

Other Forms of Cross-Training

There are countless other forms of cross training you can incorporate into your training schedule – cycling is a pretty popular one. Many runners have other sports and hobbies they already do, which they incorporate into their training. If you're looking for cross training ideas, you should try to think of activities that are a good cardiovascular work-out, but are relatively low-impact (in order to minimise the chances of injury). So, things like cycling, badminton and swimming are in, martial arts are probably out.

RACER PROFILE: RYAN SANDES

Ryan is considered one of the world's leading ultra-trail runners.

He is the first person to win all the four races in the 4 Desert Series and in 2013 became the first person to ever win an ultra trail race on all seven continents.

Ryan went on to win the 2011 edition of the Leadville 100 miler mountain race in Leadville, Colorado, setting the 3rd fastest time in the history of the race and the fastest time by a non-American - it was his first 100 miler.

He's involved with a number of philanthropic ventures and is an ambassador of the prestigious Laureus Foundation and special mention about his phenomenal career was made at the International Laureus Awards in Abu Dhabi.

In 2016 he launched his autobiography, Trail Blazer which has been a worldwide success.

You first rose to attention with your killer performance at the 4 Deserts events – what was it about stage races that first appealed to you?

The appeal of stage racing is the whole adventure of it and the community and getting to spend six or seven days with a whole bunch of like-minded people and just sharing that experience with them and just being completely removed from the rest of the world is pretty cool. I just really enjoy the multi-day, I guess you get to experience the race a lot more and meet a lot of people/

How much did your pack weigh at the start of a typical 4 Deserts race?

When I first started doing these it weighed around 11kg, and by the later ones I got it down to around 8kg. Having some experience and knowledge meant I could cut down on unnecessary things.

What advice would you give to someone preparing for their first ever stage race?

Prepare specifically for the race conditions. Get to know exactly what kind of gear you are going to use and do some of your longer training runs with the gear. Really get used to the gear and the race conditions – training in as close to the real race conditions has worked for me.

For stage races – do you have any unusual things / 'secret sauce' tips you use that helps get you through the week?

I don't have any secret recipes or anything like that, I just try to go as lightweight as possible – although I don't try and go too lightweight on my food, I always go as lightweight as I can with my gear, because you really need fuel to keep you going. I've also found stuff like just staying hydrated helps. Stock cubes and drinking soups from those have really worked for me. Otherwise there's no real secret formula. I've seen guys with olive oil and parmesan and things...you've just got to find what works well for you and have some variation.

How has the gym played a part in your training?

I think strength work is really important in preventing injuries. Doing some strength work before you go and do a big block of training is really important. It almost bulletproofs you – it makes you more resistant and prevents any injuries. It has worked well for me in keeping everything in balance – you have to work on making your muscles and body strong, because you take a lot out of it when you run.

How do you prepare mentally for a long, gruesome running event?

It's important to realise and remember why you're doing it, and focus on the positives. I always try and break a stage race down into mini-goals rather than thinking about the days ahead. Even when it gets tough, I just focus on the next checkpoint, or next sand dune, or next rock – just really breaking it down mentally into bite-sized chunks. Being able to run in some awesome places helps keep my mind on the positive side too.

How does your other sports – surfing, for example – balance with your ultrarunning?

It's been quite hard to fit too much else in with my running. Definitely I don't get to do as much surfing as I like to do. I still do a bit of mountain biking. For me its all about being out in nature, be it running, mountain biking, hiking or surfing so as long as I get that kind of fix I'm happy.

How does your preparation for a stage race vary compared to a single day event?

It's quite different. For a 100 miler I do more mileage, but for a stage race I'll do more training with a heavy pack and more race specific training. So for example I'll do blocks of training where I'll do four medium distance runs of 3-5 hrs, four days in a row to mimic race conditions.

4. TRAINING PLANS

A training plan can be a great tool when you're preparing for a stage race. A good plan will give your training schedule structure and allow you to gradually build up your endurance.

Not everyone needs a training plan - many stage racers already know that they'll go for a 2hr long run every weekend, a couple of 10 km's through the week and a gym session if they can squeeze it in. If you're in this camp then that's great, but I know that many less experienced runners have benefitted from a schedule like the one outlined below:

Having a stage race training plan can help you in the following ways:

- They are a great motivational tool - once you have drawn up your training plan, you no longer have to decide when you are going to work out, or what you're going to do - the decision has been made for you already. A training plan takes any 'decision fatigue' out of the process.

- A training plan allows you to structure your mileage increases. Say, for example, you are following the 10% rule. This means your mileage will increase by no more than 10% each week - this 'rule of thumb' is an effective way to prevent overtraining and burnout / injury. This is much easier to implement and track when done with a training plan.

- With a training plan, you can schedule days off for specific things, and move your training to suit. You can also plan out how you are going to taper, schedule in rest days, your cross training, etc. For those who enjoy recording and studying their work-outs, training plans are great.

Over at marathonhandbook.com, I've provided a link to an Excel-based training plan spreadsheet which you are free to download and customise however you like. It's also in the Appendix of this book. It incorporates all the elements I discuss and recommend in this chapter.

Build Endurance, Don't Focus on Pace

Pace training is a big deal for marathons, ultra-marathons and one-day events. When it comes to stage races, it's not such a big deal (unless you are aiming for a podium place, that is). In stage races, **endurance** trumps pace every time.

The key to a successful stage race is consistency - whether that's walking, running, or a blend of the two. In a normal marathon, you can push your body well beyond it's comfortable limits for a few hours - after all, you can spend the next week relaxing. In a stage race, the opposite is true. You want to move at a pace which you can maintain for most of the week.

With this in mind, I don't recommend worrying too much about your minutes per mile when preparing for a stage race. Instead, I'd look at doing your run training at a comfortable pace, where you push yourself only to the level of slight discomfort. Another way of describing this would be to call it a 'conversational' pace - a speed at which you could hold a conversation.

The truth is that most stage race runners don't over-analyse things like pace. Who cares if you can run at 10km/hr for the first two days, if it means you are limping by day four?

Focus on building up the time on your feet, and your body's ability to keep going after hours of running - speed is secondary.

Peak Mileage

What should be your peak mileage during training?

This depends on a lot of factors, mainly how fit you were when you started training, how much time you have to train, and what condition you want to be in at the start line.

A good rule of thumb is that prior to your stage race, you should have completed:

- At least one 50km run (preferably 60-70km)
- Two back-to-back long runs of around 42 km on consecutive days.

Tapering for Stage Races

First off, why taper?

U.S. mountain-running champion Nicole Hunt sums it up as follows:

Tapering helps "bolster muscle power, increase muscle glycogen, muscle repair, freshen the mind, fine-tune the neural network so that it's working the most efficiently, and most importantly, eliminate the risk of overtraining where it could slow the athlete down the most . . .studies have indicated that a taper can help runners improve by 6 to 20%".

The length of your taper depends on your underlying athletic ability, and the amount of training you typically do.

I'd typically look to reach the peak of my training around 3-4 weeks before the start of the stage race, and start to wind things down from there. I decrease my mileage incrementally each week and replace running and high-intensity training with swimming and things like yoga or light stretching.

Tapering Checklist:

- Mileage. Each week of your taper you should decrease your weekly mileage by 20-35%.

- Long Run. These should decrease in length significantly – if you peaked at 30 miles, then your next long run should be around 20 miles, then 12 miles, then an 8 miler a week before the race.

- Conditions. Avoid steep hills, rough terrain or anything unnecessarily challenging that could lead to injury.

Training Plan - Download Here

I've put together a six-month stage race training plan which you can download at the link below. I've also included it as an appendix to this book.

It's Excel-based and fully customisable.

The idea is that you can adjust the workouts to suit your fitness level, goals and schedule.

I hope it's of some guidance to you, but don't take it as gospel - every stage race runner approaches training in totally different ways, I've just tried to capture a good general form and share it.

If you have any questions or comments about the training plan, please let me know (hi@marathonhandbook.com)

Download the Stage Race Training Plan here – http://www.marathonhandbook.com/trainingplans

Some notes on the training plan:

- The training plan is over six months, so starts off quite lightly (three or four 10km runs per week).

- As pace isn't essential for stage race training, I have not included any pace recommendations and mainly made the runs time-based as opposed to distance based. The one exception to this is the long runs on Saturdays, which I have given set distances to cover - this is to ensure you reach the criteria of completing certain distances in preparation.

- Your weekends will be busy. I've scheduled the longest weekly runs for Saturdays, and a shorter run for Sundays. This is called running "doubles" - doing back-to-back long runs to get your body used to running long distances on tired legs.

- I've scheduled two cross training days per week, and one rest day per week. If you wish, feel free to take two rest days and only cross train once.

- I've assumed a taper of 4 weeks. This should suit most stage racers, though the more experienced runners may wish to have a shorter taper.

Download the Stage Race Training Plan here –
http://www.marathonhandbook.com/trainingplans

RACER PROFILE: CYNTHIA FISH

Cynthia Fish became one of the first women to complete the '4 Desert Grand Slam Plus' in 2016, completing five 250km races in a calendar year.

She has also completed several other stage races, such as the Global Limits races.

Cynthia walks her stage races - she is consistently 'near the back', but also has a consistent pace and strategy that works very well! She enjoys spending time during the races taking in the scenery, getting to know her fellow runners better and treating the whole thing as an opportunity.

You are unlikely to come across a more positive person in a campsite.

Hi Cynthia, you're a celebrated 'turtle' - tell me a bit about the benefits of taking it slower.

The hours between 3pm and dark are my favourite time to be outside- it's getting cooler, the light is changing, perhaps getting crisper, the sun is setting with all the changes that brings- it is my magic time. (I don't object to a good sunrise either, I just resent getting out of my warm bed to see it.) That end of time day is also the most peaceful in my head- I've pretty much wrestled my own demons, and solved a few of the world's problems, so my mind is fairly still. No chattering voices upsetting the steady tic tic tic of the poles.

It is also a time when the competitors are the most spaced out, so you often really feel solitary, alone with the world around you. One of the great features of the races is the alternating aloneness on the course, and the company in camp, so being out there by yourself is a feeling to be cherished and treasured, perhaps even a little indulged. Finally, it's the welcoming sound of the camp chatter. I was probably a sheep dog in an earlier reincarnation. I am strangely comforted by the fact that most of the racers are safe in camp. I can usually hear camp before I get there, so it's a bit of a transition moment from alone to together as I approach.

Any 'secret sauce' tips / quirky things you do to help you during stage races?

Over time I have collected a small number (read lightweight) objects or foods that have made the races more comfortable. I started with a silk scarf that I find super handy to use as a bandana, a neck warmer, a hand warmer... I sleep with it instead of a scratchy buff if it's cold, and I will often keep it on for the first few kilometres of the day.... it's just a little taste of soft that feels nice.

I added a very thin, very light (about 50 grams) sleeping mat.

I just roll it out and voila- some protection against the chill, the wet, the prickly bushes or the rocks- without the time and effort to blow up the inflatable mat, which I also bring. The roll out mat is especially pleasurable during my golden hour- the time I use to recover with my feet up and my recovery drink and snack in hand. I unclip it, roll it out, grab the food and voila! instant comfort. An hour later, I am ready to inflate the mat, but for that one hour. bliss…. It also protects the blow up map from particularly rocky bits, so it's also a bit of insurance.

I wear a pair of biking shorts over my compression leggings. The shorts have pockets in them and I carry my headlamp, my Kleenex, my hand sanitizer, and other bits and bobs. I also carry a really lightweight grocery bag, in which I put the day's dinner and breakfast items, and my bowl and cup and spork. Again, I sort out the food once, and I never have to rush back to the tent to get something I might have forgotten. Similarly, I stash my hat and my mitts in my warmest jacket- I figure if I need the hat and mitts or jacket, then I will shortly need them all.

How do you approach a stage race - what's your strategy at the start of the week?

When I was getting ready for my first race, I rehearsed each moment within the race, trying to figure out ways to make those moments flow as smoothly as possible. How to snack on the trail, where to put the snacks, how to fill the water bottles without getting water all over my front, how to lay out my mat, where to put my blister kit and how to take off my socks and shoes beside the trail. Each time I went out to train, I went over and over in my mind all the scenarios I could imagine and tried to MacGyver myself out of them.

Each race starts the same way. I wonder what on earth I am doing there. I question every decision in my life that led me to this moment. And then I smell the camp fire, lay out the sleeping bag, look up at the stars... pure happy.

What was the biggest challenges, or scary moments, of the 4 Desert Grand Slam Plus?

The scariest moment was realizing that I had six stitches in my knee from a fall on day 2 and several river crossings yet to do on the first race of the 5. Once I finished that race, upright and without an infection, the potential lions in the Namibian desert, the possible frostbite in Antarctica, the salt flats of Atacama, nothing was ever to going to scare me again. And when I had to walk 4 kilometres through a sandstorm after the end of the Long March in the Gobi, from pink flag to pink flag, with eyes streaming, I wasn't scared, I was just determined not to lose sight of the reflective tape. The most difficult (and exciting) part was travelling so much in such a short period of time to so many exotic corners of the world. Physically, resting between the races was important. Each race was tough, and cumulatively it was hard on the system, but knowing that I was going to race over the ten months, I took it easy- always keeping something inside for the last 10km.

What advice would you give to someone preparing for their first ever stage race?

You need a small music machine with some good dance music and a couple of hours of podcasts on some arcane but interesting subject. You need walking poles. Research tasty snacks. Fats are very important.

Do as many back to back long training days as you can. Walk as many kilometres as possible, everyone underestimates the amount of time they will be walking on the trail. And hip flexors get surprisingly sore surprisingly quickly.

But the most important thing is to practice practice practice with your gear. Be familiar with your gear and practice packing and unpacking it in the dark, with a head torch when you are tired. Eat the food you are planning to take two meals in a row. The only element of surprise should be the terrain. Confidence in your kit, and confidence in your ability to be able to try to make the cut-offs is what training is all about. Time spent on that at home means that your race is more pleasurable.

What was it about stage races that first caught your eye?

I started doing ultra-marathons because I am too slow to race marathons and I didn't want to race a horse. I like being outside. I like being off the grid and alone with my thoughts and beautiful landscapes. I like pushing myself hard, but I am comforted by the safety net the races give in terms of support and medical care. I didn't know I liked to sleep on the ground. And I didn't know I was good at it. Rocks don't bother me. The training regimen at home involves a fair amount of napping. Except for the fairly gnarly black toe nails at the conclusion of the race, it's all a bit of a walk in the park... kind of.

And you just keep signing up for more!

Obviously, I have a bit of an ultra addiction. I only started this sport 5 years ago, and I have averaged four ultras a year which is by any standard a lot. I like who I am when I do the race, and I like the person it has helped me be between the races. I worry less, have more confidence and patience, I feel fitter and stronger than I ever have before. Excellence doesn't have to mean podium, it can also mean putting your own best effort together and seeing where it gets you.

5. GEAR + EQUIPMENT

This section looks at every piece of clothing, running gear and other items you might take with you on your race - both the necessary and the optional. The format and rules of your race will dictate what you have to take.

<u>Self-supported races</u> mean that you have to carry everything in your pack for the whole week - this means you need to focus on sourcing items that are fit for the job while weighing as little as possible and also being as small as you can get away with. It also means that you need to find a reliable and suitable backpack that can fit all the gear you are bringing.

In a <u>supported race</u>, you only have to run with a small amount of mandatory equipment each day, so your gear requirements are different. You also need to find a suitable backpack - but this time you want one that is as small as possible.

In this chapter, **I've chosen to focus my equipment advice on self-supported races**. The reason is that equipment selection for self-supported races is critical and plays a big part in your race preparation. Also, most of the equipment advice I've given for self-supported races is also relevant to supported races. Later in the chapter there's a section of additional advice specifically for supported races.

Note: In this section I make a few explicit recommendations for particular products and pieces of equipment. I'm not affiliated with any of these companies in any way - this advice is based on my experiences, research and conversations with other stage race runners. In some instances, there is simply one or two products that are much better suited to the requirements of a stage race than other items on the market, so for the sake of being practical I have steered you towards them.

Making an Equipment List

Having a good equipment list is a key part of stage race preparation, whether you are running a self-supported race or a supported one.

I find that by far the best way to track my equipment when planning for a stage race is with a spreadsheet. Not only does it allow you to adjust the list as much as you care, but you can easily sum the weight of all your gear and figure out how much your pack is going to weigh. You can also do neat things like total your calories every day.

In the appendices of this book I've shared example equipment lists for both self-supported races and supported races.
I've also made these example lists available for download over on marathonhandbook.com - go to the stage races page and you'll find the resources section.
Note that they are formatted for Microsoft Excel and are unprotected, meaning you can customise them however you see fit.

The equipment lists I've shared on are the ones I've developed over several races for my own use over the years, and have since shared with many friends who have used them to prepare for stage races.

Finally, I include advice on how to minimise the weight of your backpack - this is particularly aimed at self-supported runners. By analysing every piece of gear you carry, you can seriously cut down on the amount of weight you have on your back at the start of your race. If you're well prepared, your backpack shouldn't weigh more than 10 kg at the start of a regular self-supported stage race.

Running Shoes

Your running shoes are the most important piece of gear you'll take with you on your stage race.

The goal of your running shoes is to get you to the finish line in comfort, without any foot-related issues.

Hopefully you've already identified a brand and type of shoe that you're comfortable running long distances in which don't give you any issues. However, it's not uncommon, especially if you haven't been running long distances for very long, to struggle to identify a shoe that's suitable. Remember - your feet change shape as your running develops. They actually become more toned, like a fine-tuned instrument - and they will grow a little bit longer. So, it's worth bearing in mind that your shoe requirements can and will change as your running develops.

When it comes to running for several days in stage races, some specific questions you might want to look at are:

- What's the terrain going to be like, and are my current shoes up to the job?
- Do my current shoes give enough cushioning for day-after-day of running?
- Are my current shoes big enough if my feet swell and grow a little as the week goes on?

If you are running a **supported race** with a drop-bag, remember you can always **carry a second pair of shoes** with you and alternate as the week goes on. Self-supported runners, on the other hand, can't really afford the luxury of a second pair of running shoes - so need to choose one good pair of shoes before the race starts.

Which Models are Popular?

OK - so if you are on the hunt for a pair of running shoes for a stage race, one place to start is to look at what brands and models are popular in stage races. The problem is that footwear is such a personal choice, with everyone having different foot shapes and running styles - there is no 'one shoe fits all' answer to this one.

Having said that, some brands are definitely more popular than others on the stage race circuit - Hoka One Ones, for example, are a maximalist shoe with loads of cushioning that get many through long races. Salomons are perennial favourites, as are Brooks. Meanwhile most mainstream shoe companies such as New Balance have released shoes designed specifically for ultra-running, such as their Leadville shoe.

How to Choose Running Shoes

If you really are lost and haven't identified a pair of running shoes for your stage race yet, then the best thing you can do is hunt out a dedicated running shoe store in your area. A running shoe store with knowledgeable staff is worth its weight in gold to an ultra-runner.

Once inside, the staff will be able to guide you in choosing running shoes. A good running store assistant will want to know a host of information before looking at a good shoe for you – your running experience, your current mileage, injury history (what it is, where it is, what aggravates it) and shoe history. Remember to make it clear exactly what you are going to be using your shoes for - i.e. training for and running a stage race - so the shop assistant can factor this in.

Trying on Running Shoes

The one way to truly know that a shoe works for you is to try it on, and then go for a run with it.

Things to remember before you leave home:

- Take your running socks with you. If you don't have a pair, look to try and buy socks in the store – then use these when trying on running shoes. Some running stores provide socks for trying the shoes, but you should be using the socks you plan to run with.

- If you use orthotics, insoles, or thick socks with your shoes normally, bring them with you when testing shoes.

- Ladies, don't forget a sports bra as the gait analysis will have a bit of running.

Some tips for trying the shoes in the store:

- **Comfort is king.** More than any other possible factor, a shoe that feels right is the one for you. If a shoe rubs or irritates you in the store, that will only get exponentially worse when you go out for a run with them.

- Don't assume you know your size– every brand varies slightly. And in stage races, your feet can swell. If you are relatively new to distance running, your feet are going to grow a little during your training, so you need to keep this in mind. Normally, you want a thumb space between the longest toe and the shoe box - however, for your stage race you may wish to consider going either ½ or one full shoe size bigger to allow for swelling. When your feet swell, the repetitive motion of the toe hitting the toe box leads to sore toes / lost toenails.

- A slightly more spacious toebox is great for your stage race - feet swell and get cramped, so you'd rather have a little bit too much room rather than not enough.

- The shoes should NOT give friction, pain, discomfort or feel too solid / hard. If you experience any of these, these are not the shoes you're looking for.

- Overall feel. Get up and walk around, if the shop has some little ramps go and see how the feet move inside the shoes when going up and down hills.

- Trial them. You should always try running with the shoes on, preferably not on the treadmill – but occasionally this is unavoidable.

- In the end, listen to your gut – don't buy a shoe you don't feel 100% comfortable in. If the staff aren't listening to your needs, you can find another store.

It's important to train in your running shoes for a few weeks before your stage race. This helps to break in the shoes, and let's you trial them out before going to the event.

Remember that some tough-terrain environments can be hard on your shoes. For example, in the Atacama the lightweight EVA that is on the bottom of many HOKA shoes can get completely destroyed by the rocks. In this case, it is better to go with a tougher soled trail shoe.

Clothing

In this section, I look at all the items of clothing you'll take with you on your stage race. Some are obviously mandatory (socks, for example) while others will be dependent on race conditions and your preferences (waterproof layers, etc.).

Running Shirt

Your running shirt is a key part of your armoury - and although it might seem like it can be hard to get a shirt wrong, there are several factors to consider when picking out a shirt for your stage race:

1. Material

Two important criteria are that your shirt should be moisture-wicking (draws sweat away from your body) and quick-drying. This means that **Polyester and nylon are in, cotton is probably out.** When cotton gets wet - be it from an icey-cold puddle in the Arctic circle, or your sweat in the Sahara, it tends to retain that moisture, so you end up with a heavy, wet shirt. Merino wool can be great for cooler events.

(The one drawback with polyester is that the bacteria in your sweat hangs around in it, even after washing, so they can start to smell a bit faster than other materials.)

2. Sleeve Length

Long-sleeved shirts can provide extra protection from the sun on warm days, or can keep you warm on colder days, so take this into consideration and gauge the conditions you're likely to experience on your run. Even in hot countries, I tend to wear a long-sleeved thin shirt which can help keep the sun off, and I can roll up the sleeves whenever I want.

3. Thickness
In cold weather, you may choose to run with two layers, or find a shirt with an inner liner that helps wick away sweat. If running in warm or hot conditions, then go for an ultra-light shirt - any extra thickness is just going to heat you up and add weight.

4. Sun Protection
If you are going to be running in any kind of sunlight, be it deserts or mountains, I recommend finding a shirt with a UPF rating. Pick your UPF rating to suit the conditions.

5. Non-chafing Seams
If you're buying a shirt from a reputable running company, these shouldn't be an issue. **Always do your dress rehearsal** before a big run though, regardless who made your shirt – the last thing you want is uncomfortable rubbing ruining your big day. Remember that if you are prone to chafing, apply Vaseline or another lubricant (more on this later).

6. Compression Shirts
Compression shirts have become increasingly popular in the past few years. Despite their popularity, many runners can't actually quantify exactly what it is that the compression gear does to enhance either performance or recovery.

Some online articles will tell you that compression wear has no effect on performance while running – others say that when compression is used correctly, it can improve venous return and help oxygenate working muscles. However, in the case of distance running, this so far seems to have only a very slight increase in performance (1 – 2%). So, I wouldn't recommend shelling out your cash for compression clothing if you just want to run that little bit faster.

Some people like the feel of compression wear while running – if you're one of these people, then go for it! Minor secondary benefits to running with compression wear is that it can keep you warmer, and reduce chafing.

7. Colour
Lighter colours absorb less heat from the sun, so white is never a bad idea in sunny climates. Lighter colours are also *more* visible at night-time, which may be worth bearing in mind. Same goes for shirts with reflective sections.

8. Accessory Pockets
There are a few shirts on the market with pockets built in at various places, usually around the lower back, for stashing your gels / salts / keys in. These can be useful in runs where you're lacking storage space and don't want to take a big pack. As always, train with the shirt beforehand and make sure the pocket load doesn't bounce around, chafe, or rub.

Running Shorts

Here's what to consider when selecting running shorts:

1. Material
You need something that is moisture-wicking (draws sweat away from your body) and quick-drying. Like shirts, polyester and nylon are good options.

2. Length
Not that I'd recommend committing sins against decency, but shorter shorts can make a difference – especially in heat. The longer the shorts, the more heat and moisture will hang around your nether regions. This leads to discomfort, chafing and rashes - do yourself a favour and buy shorts that give yourself plenty of breathing space.

3. Liner and Seams
These exist so you don't have to wear underwear, thus preventing chafing. However, when running long distances it is recommended to also apply a lubricant, like Bodyglide, down there. If you're buying shorts from a reputable running company, chafing seams shouldn't be an issue. Always do your dress rehearsal before a big run though, regardless who made your shorts.

4. Pockets
If you can get a pair of shorts with a small zip-pocket (preferably right at the back), then go for it. The additional weight and cost of getting the pocket is worth it for being able to easily store and access a couple of gels, salts, iPods, etc. on runs when you don't take a pack.

5. Compression Shorts
As mentioned in the shirts section, the effectiveness of compression gear seems to depend on who is wearing it. Many people enjoy the 'lightly massaging' feeling of

wearing compression shorts, and feel it aids with muscle recovery.

Minor secondary benefits to running with compression wear is that it can keep you warmer, and reduce chafing (but hopefully you've already eliminated the possibility of chafing using other methods).

Running Socks

Socks are easily overlooked, but they are probably the second-most important piece of kit, right after your shoes. Poor sock choice can lead to all kinds of foot conditions. Some common issues caused by incorrect sock choice include: blisters due to friction, moisture, heat and toes rubbing. Getting a good pair of socks is essential for your comfort during the race, and the socks have to be suited to both the runner and the race conditions.

Some runner's feet sweat more than others, and some runners prefer thicker - or double layered socks. Furthermore, heat, humidity and water crossings all lead to wetter socks - which you have to account for when choosing which socks to take. Finally, you want to consider *how many* pairs of socks to take...all is discussed below.

1. How to Minimise Blisters

Blisters need three things to propagate – heat, friction and moisture. You can minimise moisture by **using socks designed to 'wick' away sweat**, and you can avoid friction by buying **socks that fit your feet well**, stopping them from folding or clumping up then rubbing. Another tip for avoiding friction is to coat the blister-prone part of your feet with a **lubricant** like Bodyglide. Vaseline does work too, but tends to stick in gooey clumps that can attract dirt and sand. Many runners tape their feet - and individual toes - using **paper tape**. This form of pre-emptive preparation can prevent rubbing that leads to blisters, but as always practice doing this at home so you know what works for you, rather than trying it when you turn up to the race.

However, no matter how much you prepare, blisters are often practically unavoidable. Many veteran stage racers simply accept that they are going to get blisters, and learn how to mitigate their effects rather than prevent them completely.

2. Toe Socks

Toe socks (such as the *Injinji* brand) have become increasingly popular in ultra-running circles – they're the socks that are kinda like gloves, with a separate little section for each of your toes. By isolating each individual toe, they eliminate the risk of toes rubbing together and creating blisters in that region. It's a fairly simple solution that has worked very well for me in all my stage races. Not everyone loves toe socks, and they are more expensive than regular socks, so I'd recommend buying a pair well in advance of your race and trying them out before committing to them.

3. Double Layers

Double-layered socks can reduce friction between the sock and the foot, thereby reducing the chances of blisters. Double layered socks are obviously thicker than regular socks, which leads to more sweating and heat which some people dislike - but these are still very popular in stage races. If you don't use them already, I'd only recommend trying double-layered socks if you are having ongoing blister issues which are not resolved by using lubricant / getting properly fitting shoes and socks.

4. How Many Pairs of Socks to Bring?

This is a relevant question, and the answer depends on your race conditions and your personal preference. Many people enjoy the psychological feeling of putting on a fresh pair of socks every day, even if they're really not necessary.

If you are running a **supported race**, there's nothing stopping you from packing a fresh pair of socks for every day in your camp bag - and even carrying an additional pair during the run, in case you come across any water crossings.

For **self-supported races**, taking a fresh pair of socks for every day is more of an extravagance - they take up a bit of precious weight and space in your backpack. In a typical stage race, I'll take two or three pairs and rotate them. This means that if a pair gets wet or very dirty, I can wash them in the evening and dry them overnight - if they don't dry overnight, I pin them to the back of my backpack and let them dry out the following day. Many runners turn up to a stage race and run the whole thing in the same pair of socks - it really is personal preference.

So, things to consider when counting out your socks are:

- How important to you is it to have a fresh pair of socks for every stage?

- How many days have water crossings?

- If there are water crossings, are you comfortable continuing with wet socks, or would you rather stop and change into a dry pair?

- Is the climate hot and dry enough that you can wash and dry dirty socks overnight?

If you only have a few pairs of socks be sure to take them out and hang them up as soon as you get to camp. It may seem like there are more important things to do, but waking up in the morning to damp socks is the worst.

Hats and Buffs

Running with a hat can be a preference, but most runners will throw one on to keep the sun off their face and out of their eyes. During stage races, you're inevitably going to be outside for several hours every day, and it's very likely there will be sun - whether you're in Iceland or Morocco.

If the sun is going to be out, take a hat. If you're out for a few hours, that's a lot of sun exposure. Covering your head and face can keep you shaded and also psychologically keep that "I'm getting baked here" feeling away.

I strongly recommend hats that give total coverage! If you're running in the midday sun, a baseball cap can't cover your face *and* your entire neck.

There are a few choices for total coverage. The French Legionnaire's-style hat ticks all the boxes, but can garner some funny looks (they're basically a baseball hat with a long cover sheltering your neck from the sun), they can also get pretty warm, as they create a pocket of humidity behind your neck with no ventilation.

A soft, wide-brimmed hat with a neck-string works very well – and can even be filled with water and dunked over your head at aid stations. Google 'outdoor hat' or 'wide brimmed hat' to get some good options.

Hats can help absorb some sweat, but I also recommend taking a buff to efficiently wipe away your sweat from your head. You can choose to wrap this around your forehead, your neck, or (like me) keep it wrapped around one wrist, ready to wipe away sweat.

Sunglasses

Running-specific sunglasses can cost over US$200.

The good news is that you don't always have to buy these, and you may well already have a suitable pair of sunglasses for your stage race. While it's nice to have a pair of 'sports' sunglasses, the cost implications of buying them often make them hard to justify when compared to your existing pair of Raybans.

Here is the different criterion to consider when assessing whether a pair of sunglasses is suitable for your stage race:

1. UV protection
UVA and UVB protection should be the baseline requirement when shopping for new shades, regardless of whether they are for stage races or everyday use.

2. Comfortable when running
Do they stay fixed to your head while running? The goal here is to have a pair of sunglasses which you forget you are wearing, even in a race.

3. Preventing Fogging
Fogging is when your sunglasses get all steamed up. This is caused by the layer of evaporated sweat near your body meeting the (usually cooler) outside air temperature, and causing the moisture to condensate - on your lenses. It's apparently at its worst on cool and damp days.

Sunglasses that hug your face and provide little air circulation will fog up the fastest. So, if fogging is an issue for you, try and buy a pair of sunglasses which sit off your face a little and allow circulation, or have some form of ducts that encourage air to circulate behind the lenses.

There are now products such as *Cat Crap* which you apply to your lens and it discourages fogging (it gives them a small electrical charge which somehow prevents excessive condensation). But really for a stage race you're looking to prevent fogging by buying the right sunglasses on day one, rather than fixing it later by bringing along an extra product.

4. Weight

When preparing for a self-supported race, it's only right to weigh every single piece of gear. The good news when it comes to sunglasses is that there is a near-negligible difference between a pair of ultra-light sports shades and your buddy's new Ray-ban Wayfarers, so don't let this play a factor when the salesperson is giving his sales pitch.

Gaiters

Gaiters are designed to prevent sand, dirt and other debris from entering your shoe. They fix onto your shoes and come in a few different designs.

Gaiters are certainly not required for every type of stage race - however, if you are venturing into the desert (Marathon des Sables, some of the 4 Deserts races) then some form of gaiter is recommended - though it's surprising the number of runners who go without them. Running up and down sand dunes can fill your shoes with sand, and any piece of debris inside your shoe can lead to rubbing and blisters very quickly.

Types of Gaiter

Many shoe brands make their own gaiters (Salomon, for example) and are designed to quickly fasten to the shoe via a strap that goes around the sole of the trainer. These are great and popular for general trail-running. For more extreme conditions like sand dunes, you want a pair of desert-style gaiters which cover the complete shoe and have a decent length to them.

Sand-baggers style (www.sand-baggers.com), covering the whole top of the shoe

Gaiter Material

You should select your gaiters dependent on the application. Most desert runners choose lightweight nylon material, such as the Rough Country Silkworm model. These are super light and don't trap in heat and moisture like thicker, more heavy-made Goretex materials. Parachute material is also very popular, given its lightweight and superior strength.

How to Secure Gaiters to The Shoe

There are three options for attaching your gaiters to your shoe: Velcro, glue and stitching. **Velcro** is a nice option in that you can remove the gaiters as you wish, but doesn't provide a true 'seamless' seal – and you still have to glue / stitch the Velcro strips into your shoe.

Gluing the gaiters to your shoe can work well, as long as you don't mess up. However, the most bulletproof, and expensive, option is to pay a cobbler to **stitch your gaiters**

onto your shoe for you. It's important to find someone that is used to doing this for running shoes and knows the importance of not leaving any loose ends inside the shoe. Obviously, this method costs a bit more (you could try this yourself, but only if you're confident you won't mess it up).

One recommended supplier and stitcher in the UK is Sandbaggers (**http://www.sand-baggers.com/**), based in Glasgow. If you send them your shoes they can supply and fit their own parachute-material, designed specifically for desert running. They regularly provide this service for Marathon des Sables runners so know what a stage race entails.

Equipment

In this section, I've broken down every piece of equipment that you will need, as well as those that may be considered 'optional'. I've discussed the relevance of every item, what you need to look for, why you need it and how to optimise its use.

I've written the section from the point-of-view of a self-supported stage race, so have included a lot of advice on how to cut down on backpack weight - at the end of the chapter I have an additional section discussion weight-saving techniques. For those of you running supported races where the equipment requirements are different, the advice here still applies - I've included a section on how to prepare for these later in the chapter too. Also included are sample equipment lists for both self-supported and supported races.

What follows is a breakdown of each piece of gear you might take with you. I've separated the information into two sections - 'mandatory' and 'optional'. Most stage races have fairly common equipment lists, but you should always check your race's requirements for what is considered mandatory and optional - don't just go by the advice in this section.

And **Mandatory means Mandatory** - the race directors publish these lists for a reason, and if you don't stick to them you will get time penalties, or even worse - not allowed to start. So, you can use the following section as an informative guide, but it is **not** your actual equipment list - that has to come from the race organisers.

Also, always remember to look for your race organiser's race-specific advice. They may have specific requirements for clothing and sleeping bag temperature rating, for example, depending on the climate.

87

For those of you preparing for the Marathon des Sables, I've included a small section on the camping stove equipment in the 'optional' section.

A note on equipment lists - I always recommend having your own equipment list spreadsheet to track and analyse what you're taking to a stage race. To this end, I've included example spreadsheets and instructions - all later in this chapter.

Note on product recommendations:
For the most part, I've steered away from product recommendations, simply because there are so many worthy products out there that it wouldn't be fair to recommend only the few good ones I've encountered. Instead I've focussed on what your selection criteria should be. Likewise, I haven't recommended any shops - a good outdoors store or online retailer will have most of what you need. In some cases, though, such as backpacks, I've made more explicit recommendations towards certain brands and products. I've only done this when there is a specific product in the category which I can swear by and which many other runners use - basically when I feel it's in your best interest for me to steer you directly towards a certain product.

Neither I personally or my website are affiliated or commercially connected with any brands, and do not benefit in any way by recommending specific products.

Mandatory Equipment

Backpack (for Self-Supported Races)

Getting a backpack specifically designed for distance running is crucial – they're designed to be lightweight, durable and fit comfortably while running.

Here's some points to consider when shopping for your race pack:

• **Comfort is number one.** The pack should sit comfortably from the moment you put it on. No weird chafing or straps irritating you. It should complement the natural shape of your back and shoulders while running, and not put excessive stress on any area. Note that different backpacks suit different runners, so be wary of buying based solely on a friend's recommendation.

• Front straps. You want at least one strap that goes across your front to further secure the pack to your body and minimise movement while you run. Most good distance running packs will come with two straps – one across the chest and one across the stomach.

• Accessibility. You don't want to be stopping during a race to remove your pack just to get a gel. You want enough front and side pockets so that you can stash everything you need quick access to – gels, snacks, race booklets, salts, camera – you name it. Waterproof pockets are a bonus, too.

• Hydration system. When shopping for a pack you've got to consider what your hydration system is going to look like at the same time. If you're going with a Camelbak, does the pack accommodate this? The pack should have a separate sleeve for a Camelbak, keeping it flush with your back. If you plan to run with water bottles strapped to your front, does the pack already have bottle holders built in, and if not, which ones are you going to buy and how are you going to secure them? Strapping water bottles to the front of your pack is a great idea and is my preferred way to carry water, but if you don't get the bottle holder secured properly you will be left with a water bottle that bounces around with every step you take. You want a bottle holder system that keeps the bottles as close to your body as possible, i.e. on the shoulder straps. Therefore, you want to test out the pack with the water bottles filled. Another plus point for having the bottles mounted to your front is that it helps spread the load between your front and your back! See the Hydration System advice in the coming pages for more on this subject.

• Size. Try and get the smallest pack you can get away with. For a typical 6-stage self-supported stage race you should be able to get everything into a 25 litre pack if you are disciplined with your equipment choices. However, if you choose to take a few luxuries, or just want a little more space then there are good 30 litre packs. And remember, your pack will become lighter and emptier after every day of the race. Remember that you can utilise the straps and tie-down sections to mount sleeping bags to the outside of your pack if required. I normally am short of space at the start of a run so have to secure my sleeping bag and flip flops onto the outside.

• Front pack. Many backpacks now come with an optional smaller pack to strap to your front. These are great for two reasons – they give you a bit more room, and they also help balance the load between your front and your back.

Popular multi-day packs include the WAA 25l ultra pack, and the OMM 25l / 32l packs. I've tried both the WAA 25l and the OMM 25l, and have enjoyed both - but the WAA 25l is now my go-to pack. It's shape is less malleable, meaning it holds it's form better even when stuffed with gear - which helps when running. I've also found that the water bottle system that comes with the pack is the best I've found - it has front-mounted water bottles that hug your body really well, and even come with extra-long straws so you can constantly sip away while running. The pack itself is only a snug 20l, but it comes with an optional 5l front pack and two generous side pockets - I've found this is sufficient for my equipment (check out the example equipment list later in this section to see what I typically pack) - although for the first couple of days I do have to mount my sleeping pad and sleeping bag to the outside of my pack.

"If picking up a backpack with a front pack be sure to run for some distance with this pack filled up to the brim. I made the mistake of not trying out a front pack for my 3rd stage race and ended up having to throw it away because I felt like it was punching me in the stomach every time it moved. This caused a lot of stress, an overfilled 20L pack, and general uncomfort for the next day until I ate through some of my food and opened up some much-needed space."
- **Brendan Funk, 4 Deserts Grand Slam runner**

Backpack (for Supported Races)

In a supported stage race, your equipment is transported between campsites. This means that while running, you only have to carry your food for the day, water and some mandatory items.

While all of the above advice for self-supported races is still applicable, you only therefore need something with a capacity of around 5-10 kg.

Most supported stage race runners use a vest or lightweight small pack. I use a vest which has two bottle holders tight against the ribs, and plenty of pockets for gels and snacks. The capacity is only 4 litres - this is enough to hold the necessary bits of kit and a thin rain jacket.

Sleeping Bag

Sleeping bags are mandatory on practically all stage races. But which to take? Read on:

•   Lightweight. Don't dig your dad's old sleeping bag out from the back of the wardrobe (unless he's an ultra-runner). It's too big and heavy. If you're carrying your sleeping bag during the race, you need to go as light as you can get away with. The weight depends on the thickness, which is driven by the minimum temperature requirements. Leading me on to our next point...

•   Temperature Rating. First, find out what the night-time temperature is like and what rating of sleeping bag the organisers recommend / has worked for other people in the past. Second, verify the night-time temperature on Google (remember to look at the month your race is being held). Now you can go sleeping bag shopping. Your criteria should be based on reputation, size, weight, temperature rating and cost. In some warm climates, you can get away with no sleeping bag, but in these situations, I recommend taking a sleeping bag liner - see below.

•   Material. Down sleeping bags are lighter than their synthetic counterparts, but if you get a down sleeping bag damp, it's going to stay damp for the rest of your race - damp=heavy. If you're going deep into humid or wet territory, you might want to therefore look towards the synthetic options.

•   Sleeping Bag Liners. These are very thin sleeping bags, sometimes used as an extra layer of insulation inside a thicker sleeping bag. However, in warm climates where you don't really need a sleeping bag you can use them for comfort, and to keep the bugs off. I recommend the lightweight silk sleeping bag liners for this application – they are super light and compact. The actual temperature in which you'd use one of these as opposed to a proper sleeping bag is subjective – it depends on the environment, if there's a breeze, etc. – so best to find out through the race organiser if they feel this is good enough before you throw out your old one. If you want an insurance policy, you can always take a couple of base layers with you to throw on before you crawl into your silk sleeping bag for the night.

Hydration System

Your hydration system is your means of carrying water on the race – be it water bottles or a more elaborate bladder system.

It's typical for race organisers to have a mandatory minimum volume - usually 1.5 or 2 litres - which you have to be able to carry at any time.

First, I'll give an overview of the options, then I'll tell you what to look out for – and why I recommend that you should probably stick to simply using bottles.

The three different ways to carry water in a stage race are:

1. Sports bottles

Mounted to the front of your pack, these are an excellent way to carry your water. It's typical to get two, one on either side to evenly distribute the weight – of a size of 500-750ml. They should be very easily accessible and easy to remove and refill at checkpoints – the last thing you want is to waste time at a checkpoint because your hydration system is awkward. Nowadays some come with extra-long rubber straws poking out of them so you can sip at them without having to remove them from their pouches. You want to practice running with them before the race, as some inferior backpacks/mounting systems don't hug the bottles to your body so well, meaning they bounce around with every step. With two bottles, you can choose to have two different drinks with you - for example, water in one and an isotonic drink in the other. Ideally you want to find a backpack with good integral bottle holders (such as the WAA 25l). The other problem with these bottles is possible spillage. Test out the straws and bounce them up and down to make sure they don't leak water while you run.

2. Camelbaks / bladders

This is a rubbery bag that stays in your backpack, with a big tube straw reaching round over your shoulder to feed you. These can be an awesome way to carry larger amounts of water when you're out on the trail – a bladder system can store 2-3l that your sports bottles can't. The disadvantages are that they can be awkward to re-fill (taking your backpack off at every checkpoint), they get unhygienic easily (how can you keep one of these completely clean if you're out in the jungle for a week?) and it's hard to gauge how much water you have left.

3. 'Platypus' style bag

These are super-lightweight little plastic bottles which come in different sizes and hold water. They aren't designed for use while running. There's typically no straw system or anything fancy, and they're usually used as a back-up system for additional capacity (see bullet point on capacity below). They can be rolled up and stashed in the bottom of a bag easily. Note that in a squeeze, an empty Coke bottle is an apt replacement.

So, here's the main things you want to consider when choosing your hydration system:

• **Capacity**. Check your race's "minimum water carrying capacity" early on during planning – this is the amount of storage you have to have. Many races set this at 2 litres, but will actually give you only 1.5 litres of water at checkpoints – they 'reserve the right' to give you up to 2 litres if they think a particular stage is gonna be really hot or arduous. In my experience, 1.5 litres every 10 km is sufficient in almost any condition. Biologically, your body (specifically the GI tract) can only normally process 700-800ml/hr - the rest will slosh around somewhere. So factoring in your running speed is important - slow walkers should take more water at checkpoints than speedy runners

Anyway, for people looking at using sports bottles – what I recommend for this scenario is to take 2 x 750ml sports bottles, front mounted for easy access – then carry a lightweight 500ml or 1l 'platypus' bottle at the bottom of your pack, in case you ever need it (unlikely). The 1l platypus I use weighs 38g so won't burden your pack. I've even seen runners use an empty plastic coke bottle to cover the capacity requirements!

- **Comfort and accessibility.** Whether your hydration system is front loaded or back loaded, you really need it to be hugging your body – or else it's going to bounce around with every step you take, especially when full. Unfortunately, there are many front-mounted hydration systems on the market which don't secure the bottles well to your body- I've bought a few of them. The only way to check this is by going for a trial run with your hydration system.

- **Visibility.** In other words, being able to see how much fluid you've got left in your hydration system. You want to easily be able to tell how much water you've got left, so you can plan your consumption between checkpoints. You don't want to accidentally drain your reservoir when you're 5km from the next aid station in the desert. Transparent front-mounted sports bottles win this one hands down over a bladder / reservoir system.

Multi-tool / knife

Some races require you to take a knife, some require you to take a multi-tool. Unless specifically stated, something like this lightweight credit-card-shaped multi-tool is all you actually need:

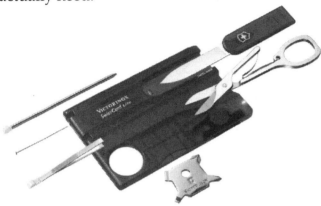

For those of you watching your weight, the above 'Swisscard' is only 26g – and you can probably lose a few more grams by discarding the bits you don't need.

Another option (depending on the mandatory requirements) is a thin Stanley blade - you can even break it in half and get it down to around 6g.

The three things you'll typically use your multi-tool / knife for on a stage race are:

1. Cutting pieces of sports tape, duct tape and sticky bandage (those tiny scissors are handy).

2. Popping blisters (use that tiny needle - or a safety pin, sterilise with a lighter + some alcohol gel first).

3. Cutting the tops off plastic bottles to make cups (knife).

Therefore, don't read too far into the knife requirements. Even though you're going into the wilderness for a week, it's fairly unlikely you'll need anything more serious than the above.

Headlamp

The headlamp is an essential piece of kit for running in darkness and also navigating campsites in the dark. Here's what you need to consider:

• Check what's mandatory. Some races just require one headlamp, some require one headlamp plus a spare set of batteries, some require a back-up torch (headlamp or hand torch).

• Sufficient brightness is important. The headlamp needs to be able to brightly illuminate the terrain 2-3 metres in front of you, in the dark. If you stick to reputable brands, it's unlikely you'll end up with something too weak – but I'd be wary of anything less than around 70 lumens.

• Lightweight is king. Especially for something that could be strapped to your forehead for several hours. And don't forget to use lithium batteries – they're lighter and last longer than regular batteries.

• A dimmed setting, or red-light setting is very useful. This is a nice feature to have for when you've finished running and are moving around a campsite. It can frustrate other runners when you look at them with your white 'full beam' in the middle of the night.

• Be aware that it can be very easy for your headlamp to get bumped against something while in your bag and turn on, draining the battery without your knowledge. Bear this in mind when checking out headlamps and try and pick up one which doesn't have an 'on' button that will easily be knocked into the 'on' position.

Blister Kit

Typically, a blister kit is mandatory for stage races. Some race directors will have specific minimum requirements for what's inside the blister kit, so check these. Even if a blister kit is not on the mandatory list, it is always worth bringing along some tape as a minimum. If you're unfamiliar with the contents of a blister kit, then check it out and get to know what you have.

A good blister kit will include some sterilised needles for draining blisters, some alcohol wipes for sanitizing the affected area, and some tape for patching over treated blisters. By the time you are lining up to start your stage race, you should have a pretty decent idea how blister-prone you are. However, it's impossible to predict how your feet will handle the strains of a stage race - especially if it's hot/wet/humid! So the advice here is be prepared and make sure your blister kit is comprehensive, even if it's not all mandatory.

"Ok so my blister kit has a safety pin, alcohol pads and some toilet paper. After a stage, I check my feet for blisters. If there is one, I put two holes on the top and two in the bottom for drainage and make sure the blister drains. I stick some toilet paper on it and keep it there as long as I can. The idea is to provide drainage and allow the skin to collapse back on the skin bed and reattach itself. The next morning, I check the blister as soon as I get up to see if it has reformed. I might do that during the night as well, if I get up. That's what I have doing for the past 20 or more races. If the skin rips off, I place second skin and Leukotape on top and keep it on till the end of the race. If the blister reforms under the leukotape, I puncture it but it's harder as you can't actually see the blister."

- **Ash Mokhtari, stage race veteran**

For further reading, the <u>absolute bible</u> for blister care is a book called '*Fixing Your Feet*' by John Vonhof. The writer has manned hundreds of race hospital tents and race checkpoints over the years, and knows exactly how to deal with every type of blister. The book is as comprehensive as you could imagine, detailing how blisters form, every possible way to prevent them and to treat them. The book is especially of interest as it is written for distance runners.

First Aid
There's usually fairly minimal requirements here – some races will ask you to take a compression bandage, while the Marathon des Sables asks everyone to take a venom pump.

You can normally expect the race doctors to carry a pretty comprehensive first aid kit, especially on the bigger races. If in doubt you can get in touch with the organisers to clarify what would be available if required.

Medication
1. Pain medication
Some form of pain medication is usually mandatory, and many runners take it regardless of if they have any pain. Many feel it helps ease any discomfort during the run and will pop one every morning as a preventative measure, or it may help you sleep if your aching muscles are keeping you up. Others will only take a painkiller if they feel they really need it – it's a personal decision.

When it comes to pain medication, the **most important thing** is to be aware of what type you're taking - as some can be harmful to you in race conditions.

Paracetamol (tylenol, anacin, panadol, etc) is a mild painkiller. Most race directors will point you towards this because it has relatively low side effects.

Ibuprofen (or Nurofen, Aspirin, Advil – any Non-Steroidal Anti-Inflammatory Drug - NSAID) is more potent, but has more identified side effects - specifically the strain on your kidneys. If you are dehydrated when you consume them (out running in the desert, say), their effect on your kidneys is magnified and in extreme conditions could lead to serious kidney issues, if not total kidney failure.

For this reason, race doctors would recommend you stick to paracetamol while out on the trail, and only hit the NSAIDs once you are home and dry, rested and hydrated.

2. Imodium

Used to treat diarrhoea. I'd recommend taking 2 or 3 pills in your pack, but only take them if required. Travelling to strange countries and eating exotic cuisine will often bring on a case of 'Delhi belly', and you never know when you'll pick something up on a run.

3. Sleeping Pills

Many runners struggle to drift to sleep after a day on the trails – whether it's restless or aching legs, too much sun, an uncomfortable sleeping surface or just a new environment – sometimes it's hard to switch off. It's optional, and the majority of runners don't usually take them, but sleeping pills can help. As with everything, it's important to try your sleeping pills before bringing them to a race – everyone is affected by them in different measures. If you're not sure, it doesn't hurt to carry a couple at the bottom of your pack which you could use as the week goes on.

For women and for anyone in general high-altitude conditions, it may be advisable to bring some iron pills as well.

Emergency Bivvy Survival Blanket / Bag

This is a lightweight sleeping bag made of a super-lightweight waterproof material. They're designed for use in emergencies - the material reflects all your body heat back to you, and the bright orange is highly visible. Their purpose on stage races is really in case you get totally lost or in trouble and need to preserve heat. Some of my friends have used them just for warmth while waiting around on cold mornings prior to a race kicking off.

Lightweight is all you're really after here, as it should remain at the bottom of your pack throughout the race. Some event organisers only require a blanket as opposed to a full bag. If a blanket is all they require, this is lighter and cheaper – have a quick look online.

Whistle, Compass and Mirror

These are all survival items that you should hopefully never have to use during a stage race. In other words, small and lightweight are your two main criteria as you'll be lugging this stuff around in the bottom of your pack for the whole race. The purpose of the whistle and mirror is to attract attention during an emergency, while the compass could be used to help you navigate if you get completely lost. Many backpacks have built-in whistles, but make sure these are acceptable with your race director - some races don't consider them as sufficient. Also, a plastic mirror is more lightweight than a glass equivalent. Outdoors stores often sell little compasses with built-in mirrors.

Eating Vessel (Bowl / Cup / Dish)

Alright, here's one you've got to plan round, based on what you are eating. Remember that those dehydrated meals can be consumed straight from the bag - if you choose to keep the bags. Six days-worth of those robust bags adds up in weight to quite a few grams - if you can decant the contents into smaller ziplock bags, you can save yourself a good amount of weight. The ziplock bags are a little easier to pack too - the robust heatproof packaging of the dehydrated meals is pretty firm and takes up a lot of room in your pack. So - what to bring as an eating vessel if you're not going to eat from the bag?

Many people bring some sort of lightweight eating vessel for their meals, soup, tea, coffee, etc. There are rubber telescopic bowls and cups these days that are lightweight and take up minimal room. Likewise, a titanium cup is lightweight and super-robust. In races where you have to heat your own water (such as the Marathon des Sables) a titanium cup is recommended. Although they take up some space, you can use them to store other small pieces of camp equipment while in your pack.

A favourite space-saving method is to just use one of the plastic water bottles provided by the organisers, first removing the top half with your knife and leaving you with a makeshift bowl.

This works well, but some races are stopping bottled water altogether these days and moving towards big plastic reservoirs, so check ahead before relying on this method. The most minimalist and least pleasant option is to use a ziplock bag for eating and drinking from.

Safety Pins

These are just required for pinning your number to your shirt and bag, along with any race patches they might give you. You can also use a safety pin to pop your blisters when in a fix, just sterilise it first (see next point).

Lighter

This occasionally crops up on mandatory equipment lists. The only thing you're likely to use it for, unless you've got to make a campfire, is sterilizing a safety pin to pop a blister.

Eating Utensil

A camping spork is the best option here. They're light and robust. Titanium ones are ideal.

Personal Care

This covers toiletries and the essentials for life out on the trail. Let's break down every item you're likely to take, and discuss what to look for:

1. Disposable Towels

You typically use these for going to the bathroom, but along the way you'll find you want to use them for everything from cleaning your feet to wiping your face down. So budget appropriately and err on the side of caution – no one wants to run out of toilet paper half-way through a race.

Wet wipes are a godsend out in the jungle / desert / wherever. Moist, sanitized, cooling – what else do you need? The only problem is, since they're pre-hydrated, a week's supply of wet wipes can weigh a bit more than you'd like.

Luckily there are a couple of options for you. One is to dry out wet wipes before the race – leave them out in a dry room overnight, near a radiator if possible and they should be fairly dry by the morning. Stuff them in a ziplock bag and you're ready to roll – just throw some water on them on the trail and they're good as new.

The other great option are '**tablet towels**'– these go by different brand names, but they are tiny, super-compressed tablet-shaped cloth towels that weigh *nothing*. Soak them for a few seconds and they jump to life. They're so light you can always take a couple dozen spare and it won't affect your pack weight.

2. Alcohol Gel (hand sanitiser)

Get a tiny bottle of hand sanitizer from your local shop – 60 to 80 ml (2-3 fl.oz) is plenty for a week long run as long as you use it sensibly. For use after the bathroom, and sterilising / cleaning the area around a wound or blister.

Given that bathroom and washing facilities are typically very rudimentary on stage races, personal hygiene is very important. This is especially true in races in foreign locales. Practically every race has a few runners developing stomach issues, which really cripples your progress - if it doesn't stop you altogether. Running a stage race in perfect health is tough enough, doing it while ill is an extreme challenge. Therefore, **practice good sanitation habits as much as possible**. Alcohol gel is very effective.

3. Toothbrush and Toothpaste
Find the smallest bottle of toothpaste you can – the ones you get on planes are ideal, and have enough toothpaste to last a week.

Regarding toothbrushes, regular toothbrushes are already fairly light. If you get a compact one, such as an airline one, it can save a few grams. Some dedicated runners go to the extreme of cutting the handle off their toothbrush and just taking the brushy head bit – I'm unsure if the few grams saved really makes this worth it.

4. Sun Cream
There are few locations where you can go distance running and not bring sun cream. Always buy a high factor (SPF50 +, after all, you're not going to your race to get a tan). Look for water / sweat proof stuff (P20 is a proven, popular brand for extreme environments). For a week-long race, around 80 ml is the minimum you could get away with. Each morning, smear the cream everywhere that will be exposed to the sun. Don't forget your neck and the tops of your ears! Lip Balm with an SPF factor is never a bad idea either.

Optional Equipment

The items in this section don't usually feature on mandatory equipment lists, but are very popular and common on stage races.

I've tried to cover practically any item that someone might want to take with them, in order that first-time stage race runners don't feel they are missing anything.

Sleeping Pad

Although a sleeping pad or mat is always considered 'optional', it is one piece of gear that almost any runners would never go without. Unless you're used to sleeping rough on hard surfaces, I highly recommend taking some form of cushioning. Let's look at the two main types (foam vs. inflatable), then look at your criteria for selecting one:

1. Foam pads

These are foam pads that usually fold up like an accordion and can be secured to the outside of your pack.

They are rugged and very hard wearing – no matter what you put them through. Also, they're easy to modify and cut bits off to make them smaller and lighter. They're generally the most lightweight option around, but aren't as comfortable as an inflatable pad. They're also generally cheaper than inflatables.

During self-supported stage races, it's common to see that people have trimmed sections off their foam sleeping pad to reduce weight. Some runners find they only need enough to cover a shoulder-to-knee length, others only take enough to cover shoulder-to-hip.

When I used to use a foam pad, I always secured it to the outside of my pack. They are quite bulky so that's the best place for it. My foolproof technique for securing it to my pack was to pierce holes through the foam, so when it was collapsed I could run a piece of string strong through it in two points, then tie that to my pack.

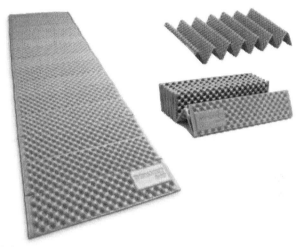

The Therm-A-Rest Z-Lite Sleeping Pad (410g full size)

2. Inflatable pads

There's no doubt an inflatable pad is comfier than a foam one. While some are self-inflating, most you have to blow up yourself – but no big deal. You'll find you probably are most comfortable when the pad is only 60-80% inflated anyway.

Inflatable pads do tend to be more expensive, and run the risk of puncture if you're not careful! However, they should always come with a patch repair kit, and it's fairly unlikely you'll do such damage that it will be unusable. Some campsites will attract things like thorns and sharp pebbles, so keep your area clear when setting up your inflatable pad.

Traditionally, deflated pads were heavier and more bulky than a foam pad. However, the below pad – Therm-A-Rest NeoAir Xlite – is only 350g (medium size) and rolls up into a sports bottle-sized bag.

From the racers I've talked to, it has become the go-to choice for sleeping packs in the last few years. I used it in my last self-supported race and found it much more comfortable than a foam pad.

Therm-A-Rest Z-Lite Sleeping Pad (350g medium size)

Some things to consider:

• Pillow. Some support for your head is essential, but in a self-supported race taking a dedicated pillow is a bit of a luxury. You can use your backpack, or put your spare clothes inside a bag and use this. I like to take a buff that I keep clean to put on top of my pack, just to avoid sleeping directly on my pack. If you decide to take a dedicated pillow, the airline neck-pillows are a great option – look for one that fastens / secures around your neck.

• Size of pad. Many people trim down their foam pad to only cover their hips to their shoulders or chest – a sort of minimum area of comfort. I recommend trying out your sleeping pad first before cannibalizing it! Inflatable pads come in different sizes, so weigh up the comfort of a bigger pad with the increased weight.

• Sleeping bag. Some people slip their foam pads inside their sleeping bags and say this is more comfortable – you might want to experiment with this.

Flip flops / slippers

Some cheap flip flops or slippers are needed on a stage race to wear after you finish running for the day. Letting your battered feet breathe is important, but you also need some form of protection.

Most runners take a cheap pair of Havaiana-style flip flops. Look for a light-looking pair – the cheaper foam versions will be lighter than the more expensive rubber ones.

Some runners advise that cheap hotel slippers are best. These are definitely the lightest option, but many hotel slippers are not that comfortable and are really flimsy – they're not designed for wearing outdoors, so may not last.

This comes down to personal preference and how much you are scrutinizing your pack weight. My advice is, if you choose to take light hotel slippers, make sure you're happy with them and maybe even beef them up with some duct tape prior to starting the race. I personally have quite big feet (UK11) and find these are a little small and mean I can only hobble around with them.

Lubricant

Lubricant can make or break your stage race. While it is in the 'optional' section of this chapter, for me it will always be a mandatory item. It is generally recommended to apply lubricant between the legs, on the feet and anywhere else you think might chafe. Vaseline does work, but is a bit gloopy and if used on the feet can attract grit and sand. Products such as Bodyglide and Pure 2skin gel are designed specifically for runners.

Lubricant is especially important if you are somewhere hotter or more humid than where you typically run.

Cooking Equipment (Marathon des Sables)

The majority of races will give you hot water at the camp sites, so this is not required. However, cooking, or at least heating your own water, features in the Marathon des Sables – so I thought I'd cover it here.

Note that some runners who are strict about weight will not take any equipment to heat water – they'll just add cold water to their dehydrated foods and let it heat up a bit in the sun.

Fuel has to be bought from the Marathon des Sables organisers, and they hand it to you at the first campsite. It is possible to use random sticks / twigs as fuel, if you're not worried about your food definitely being hot.

When it comes to choosing a cooking stove, keep it lightweight. A titanium cup, as discussed earlier, is perfect for heating water in.

Trekking Poles

Trekking poles can be a great support and are recommended if you are either:

- Planning to walk the majority of the race - they can help take the strain and load off your legs.

- Traversing a lot of technical terrain (rocky screes, sand dunes, steep hills).

Walking with trekking poles is fairly intuitive. Running with trekking poles, however, especially in technical terrain, is a skill that many people don't appreciate until they're trying to do it during a race.

Using trekking poles on technical terrain provides stability and takes the load off your legs, especially your knees.

When faced with sand dunes, trekking poles can help you scurry up the steep gradients, providing a bit of an anchor. Some runners will take a single trekking pole for such occasions.

For walkers especially, trekking poles are a great help - the longer you spend on your feet, the more you benefit from their support. You often find that runners travelling together will share a set of poles, rotating them so everyone gets the benefit.

GPS Watch

Typically, stage races are well-marked and some runners will take a GPS device for personal preference, rather than through necessity. Some features and discussion on what to consider for a GPS watch:

- Basic info and accuracy. Pace and distance covered are the most basic pieces of information any GPS device should be able to give you. This can help you anticipate the location of checkpoints and plan accordingly. However, don't assume your GPS device and the course marker's one are identical – on every race you'll find there's a runner complaining that the published stage distances are different from what their watch is telling them. Use your own GPS as a guide, but be aware there will be discrepancies between your watch and the official map.

- Navigation feature. More sophisticated GPS devices allow you to preload a route map onto them, and will display your position relative to the trail. If your race director can provide the digital GPS files for the route then this is a good option.

- Battery life. Ensure your GPS watch is going to last the length of your race – the cheaper models only last a few hours, while more expensive ones will last for over a week. Find out if power will be available at the campsites to charge them. Also note that in order to maximise battery life, you may have to change the settings to decrease the frequency of the GPS position checks. I found this out the hard way when my long-life GPS watch died six hours into a 100km race...

Electronics - Cameras / Music

I'm going to cover cameras and music players together in one section, because nowadays the best option is often to take a smartphone which does both of these features.

An **iPhone 7** is 129 grams. Consider that this includes a high-quality camera, a music player, a notebook, a GPS device and whatever other apps you might want to use on the trail. It is also your emergency phone in case you run into trouble. If you don't have charging facilities, you can keep it turned off or on in-flight mode. It's the simplest, lightest, all-in-one option.

Digital Camera. On some races, I take a digital camera instead of my smartphone in order to get better quality photos and improved battery life. Remember that lithium batteries are lighter than regular ones, and take sufficient memory cards. Also bear in mind that when you're out on the trail it can be hot, sweaty, sticky and wet – you might want to take your camera in a dedicated, small Ziplock bag.

iPod. If you're leaving your smartphone at home but still want something to listen to on the trails, go and pick up an iPod Shuffle or two. The latest ones weigh 12 grams (i.e. nothing) and clip onto any part of your kit. They have a battery life of around 12-15hrs. I load them up with either music playlists, podcasts or audiobooks and save them for when the trails get tough.

iPod Shuffle – 4th generation

Spare Shoes

Taking an extra pair of running shoes can potentially save your race if you're not confident in your main pair of shoes. Being able to switch shoes or alternate them can potentially alleviate any debilitating foot injuries or blisters.

Most runners don't take a second pair of shoes simply because they don't need them. They are confident in their shoe selection and trust they can go the full race in one pair.

For self-supported races, taking a spare pair of shoes is a real luxury that adds a lot of weight. However, if you are running a semi or fully supported race, it is worth considering throwing a spare pair of shoes in your bag – just in case.

Ziplock Bags

These could be in the 'mandatory' section – Ziplock bags are your way of keeping all your gear dry, segregated and neat. I probably use around 20 Ziplocks of various sizes during a six-stage race. I recommend keeping any clean clothes sealed in a ziplock bag. For self-supported races, you should segregate your food into daily Ziplocks. I have a Ziplock for my toiletries, a Ziplock for my camp gear, a small Ziplock with money and my phone...I even decant my dehydrated meals out of the original packaging and into Ziplocks to save some space and weight. They're versatile and will always come in handy...those filthy socks you walked through mud with? Put some water in a Ziplock bag and throw the socks in to wash them out – leave them outside to dry then store them in a Ziplock bag to keep them away from your other gear. The uses are endless, and Ziplocks really come into their own when it starts to get wet...

Large Waterproof Bag

This has two great uses and takes up zero room in your pack:

i)   if it's raining or wet, you can throw it around your pack and keep everything dry,

ii)   at the end of the race, you can throw all your stinking, worn out race gear in it, tie a knot in it, and forget about it all until you get home!

You have two options - take a robust waterproof sack to keep your things dry, or simply take a black refuse bag. The latter is much more likely to tear and not last the week.

Kinseo Tape (Rocktape, KT Tape, etc.)

Many runners will already be familiar with this stuff – the multi-coloured elastic tape you see on legs all over the country. Kinseo tape can be very effective at suspending pain while running (i.e. allowing you to continue to run through an injury without making it worse) – especially when it comes to events like ultra-marathons.

After several days of running, many runners' knees can flare up. A couple of well-applied strips of Kinseo tape can hold things together and aid alignment issues, allowing the runner continue. For my money, Rocktape has been the strongest and most durable of all brands I've tried. A few strips is relatively light and will not have an impact on your pack weight.

Massage Accessories

Trigger point balls, muscle roller sticks and foam rollers – all accessories designed for self-use to work the knots out of your body. Though it may not be so practical on a self-supported race, in a semi-supported race it's easier to justify taking something that helps work your muscles after each day's running. GRID produce a small foam roller, around 18cm in length, that could be thrown in your drop bag.

In a fix, you can use a tennis ball, racquetball, or something similar for self-supported races.

Charging Equipment

If you want to bring your own charging system, you're veering into the 'luxuries' section of the Optional Equipment category.

Powertraveller produce a range of lightweight travel options – both battery packs and solar-charging systems. Be aware that portable solar chargers usually get mixed reviews, and in the field sometimes disappoint – when they do provide charge, it's often drip-fed at a very slow rate. If you bring one, test it beforehand and don't rely on it as a bulletproof energy source.

Other

Some other small items people often bring along include **spare shoelaces, travel sewing kits and duct tape**. Unless you foresee a need for any of these, you can leave them at home.

Minimising Backpack Weight

You want to keep all gear you are running with as light as possible - the less weight you have to carry; the less energy you expend with every step. It pays off to go with the ultra-light options whenever you can.

If you can, you should get a backpack just big enough to fit everything you need in it - a big bag means excess weight. For self-supported races, one of the most important pieces of kit you should buy is one you'll end up leaving at home - a good set of digital kitchen scales.

I recommend starting a spreadsheet (or use my one as a template - see next section), digging out your scales, and weighing every piece of food and equipment that goes into your pack. This way you get to know exactly how much you're going to be carrying, and can start to scrutinize individual items for weight saving.

Some runners go nuts in analysing each item and how to trim a gram here or there - it's not uncommon to see people having broken the handle off their toothbrush, or loose straps trimmed from their backpack.

Here's a couple of tips when you're putting your inventory together:

Luxuries

For some people, this is a bag of sweets, cans of Coke, a book, solar charging station - whatever. People like to bring non-mandatory stuff that will be comforting, or remind them of home, when they're out in the desert. In my experience, a lot of first-timers do this and then find they don't need whatever they brought. Remember, on a self-supported stage you've got to cart around these things for the whole week. Plus, it tends to lead to the justification of taking more stuff, i.e. "well if I'm taking an iPod charger I might as well take that portable speaker system I got last year..."

Bringing 'generalised' equipment

Things like backpacks, pocket knives, waterproof jackets, sleeping bags - they are things we all probably have at home already. However, there's could be a 300 gram difference between the waterproof jacket you've had at the back of the closet and the ultra-light ones designed specifically for distance running. Although there is a cost associated with buying new running-specific equipment, you should analyse the weight saving vs. cost implication for each major item and see what you can do. Backpacks are another classic example - leave your old military bag at the back of the wardrobe and buy a lightweight 25l ultra-marathon bag - you'll be grateful you did towards the end of the week!

Packaging

This applies mainly to your food. Strip out any unnecessary and bulky packaging, decant foods into ziplock bags - whatever you can do to lighten the load!

Remember during training to try and get a few runs in with your pack.

RACER PROFILE: MARK ROE

Mark Roe completed several marathons, ultras and Ironman triathlons through the 1990s and early 2000s but as he became more senior in his legal career the enjoyment of those gave way to waning health because of inactivity.

After four years of doing next to nothing, hitting 224 pounds or 102 kilos on a diet of daily cake, chocolate and fizzy sodas, how did he turn this around? Mark needed a new goal to get motivated again, a bigger challenge than any he'd completed to date.

So, he decided to enter the **Marathon des Sables** and completed it in 2012, going on to document the transformative experience in his book, *Running From Shadows*.

Since then, Mark has continued to run marathons and recently completed the Global Limits Ancient Khmer Path in Cambodia, a 220km 6-day stage race.

Mark blogs about his running adventures over at www.runningfromshadows.com .

What was it about the Marathon des Sables that first appealed to you?

I'd become overweight and unhealthy and I needed a motivational kick up the backside but didn't really know what would do the trick. I'd already run 24 and 6 hour races, marathons, a few Ironman triathlons, although they were years before, so I needed A New Big Thing. I was on holiday in Majorca, a rare retreat from the office, overweight and feeling pretty crappy about myself. I'd barely moved for 4 years so I went for a run and 20 minutes later in the fierce sun and heat I was gasping, sweating like a pig and feeling sick. Then I felt even more crap, thinking *How did I get like this?!* I knew I needed to change as I was in this state and not yet 40! I looked around at colleagues several years older and thought "I don't want to end up like them." I'd heard about the MdS years before and it was always a "No way!" in my head ... but after that 20 minute jog sat on the track retching it popped into my thinking . . . so it became The New Big Thing that I needed to motivate me back into training again.

What mistakes did you make in your MdS preparation?

Plenty! And that's why I'm still training for these multi-days: there's lots to learn to keep improving. For the MdS my biggest mistake was not acclimitising to the heat enough, but that's difficult in the northern hemisphere anyway when you're plunging yourself into temperatures in the 50Cs. The other mistake was not losing more body weight: I'd lost about 28 pounds or 13 kilos by the start of the race but hadn't significantly changed my diet. I did well in the race, for a first-timer, but wonder how much more I could have achieved being lighter . . . seems silly now worrying about cutting labels off my rucksack when I still had plenty of body weight to shift! Oh, and core or general strength work in the gym: didn't do any and suffered for it. Later meeting my coach Rory Coleman taught me the importance of that.

What has been the biggest failure for you, during stage races - and how have you addressed it?

Not keeping cool at every opportunity. After the MdS I DNF'd at a stage race in Jordan and also at my first attempt at the Global Limits' Cambodia stage race. In Jordan I had some nasty stomach problems: not keeping cool wouldn't have helped but I don't think I had my electrolyte strategy sorted properly anyway. Ditto on the Cambodia race. At my second Cambodia attempt I had a wobble but the course marker, Manu Pastor, got me through that and race volunteer Meese Geert then gave me a top but blindingly obvious tip: at every opportunity, get cool! I finished the race following that advice and just got stronger and stronger. You forget the obvious when in the thick of it! Now I wonder what more I can do if I keep cool for my next race!

How do stage races influence other aspects of your life, whether personal or professional?

Well, finishing the MdS saw me change my career so it's had a major, positive impact there. With a better work-life balance I can fit in the training for these amazing experiences. It's not all been plain sailing though: I think you have to come to learn how to become an expert in managing your time. It's the only way to fit in the training along with everything else going on in life. It really is possible though: just learn what's really important and get on with it; ditch everything else.

Is it hard to find time to train sufficiently for stage races?

It can be difficult sometimes fitting it all in but it's not impossible. If you really want it, you'll find the route. It's about becoming a master of your time. I don't have kids, fortunately, but I've had several conversations along the lines of "If only you knew what it's like to have kids!" They're not the ones completing stage races. I know plenty of successful stage race runners who have kids/family/commitments who fit it all in. I remember one guy on the MdS: the only training time he had was after his shift and putting the kids to bed. So he was out at midnight with his headtorch running up and down his local hill. Getting out for a run at midnight is the real test of whether you want to train for and finish a race.

What advice would you give to someone preparing for their first ever stage race?

If you have it to lose, get rid of the body weight.

Get a thorough idea of the environment and terrain you'll be racing in: adapt your training to take this into account as best you can. Sleep more.

Ditch all the time-wasting activities in your life: ask yourself "Why am I doing this?" Training, good sleep and good diet are vital in the months up to the race, as is earning a living and managing a home. It's just one example, but I learnt that I wasn't getting much more out of life staying up to watch the 10 o'clock news for half an hour and then sacrificing a 6am gym session because I was too knackered: just glance at the headlines online instead, that's all you need to know. That's half an hour of extra sleep.

Any 'secret sauce' tips / quirky things you do to help you during stage races?

3M E-A-R Classic ear-plugs and eye mask.
Observe everything around you in the present in the minutest detail: the external focus keeps you away from the internal pains . . . and will give you vivid memories lasting a lifetime.

6. NUTRITION +

HYDRATION

"During a race, food is without doubt the topic people spend most time on and discuss the most - and it's the majority of your pack weight.

Put at least as much thought and energy into this during your training as you have for the rest of your gear.

Pack your food the smart way - one ziplock bag of food per day. You probably don't need breakfast on day 1 or dinner for the last stage. Look at the race itinerary and pack smart. The long stage might also mean more food while running and less for a solid dinner if you plan to finish at 2 AM."

- **Peter Jorgensen, veteran stage racer**

Choosing the right food for a stage race is a bit of a balance - you have to consider weight, calories, and your own appetite. There's a myriad of options out there, and there's no one menu that suits everybody. When it comes to dehydrated meals and energy gels, some runners live by them, others cannot stomach them. So, it comes down to personal preference.

In this section, I look at the various food options you have during your stage race - and offer advice on what to eat before, during and after your run each day.

The main thing the race organiser is interested in is your calorie count. They want to see that you are eating enough food to keep yourself going throughout the week. The Marathon des Sables, for example, stipulates a minimum of

2000 calories of food per day. Of course, this is the minimum and many runners take more. An example of how you might divide these calories up would be: 500 to 700 calories for breakfast, 600 during the day then 800 for dinner. I go into further detail in *what* you should eat later in this chapter.

Hydration and salts are also a big area of concern when it comes to distance running. Here, I explain why they are important, what the latest advice is on salts/water intake, and how to practically manage them during your stage race.

Food Before You Run

Your goals for eating before a running event should be:

i) eat something that will fuel your event

ii) don't try anything new or exotic

iii) don't eat anything that might unsettle your stomach.

On a self-supported race, you're limited as to what you can carry – so it's vital to get your morning food choices correct. Dehydrated meals are fairly popular, but many find their thick, stodgy texture to be too much to stomach first thing in the morning.

I tend to find that while the dehydrated breakfasts are high in calories, most of them come from a ton of milk powder - which is cloying and tough to eat first thing in the morning. Instant noodles are a popular alternative – they are a bit plainer and easier to process, while being high in calories and tasty.

Similarly, off-the-shelf instant porridge sachets can be a good source of fuel. My general advice is to eat as much as you can stomach on the morning of each stage - which may not be much.

A sachet of instant coffee or green tea can be a nice addition to your breakfast - and weighs nothing.

Food While You Run

The reason you might eat while you run is to convert food into energy to fuel you – therefore, you want to select foods that:

i) can quickly and easily be digested and turned into energy

ii) have a high calorie content – calorific value is a direct measurement of energy in food

iii) assuming you are carrying this food, you want it to be lightweight, or have the highest calorie to weight ratio possible

iv) be edible in the conditions you are running in – if you're going for a race in a hot climate, you want something you can still stomach after 4hrs in 40°C heat!

Fuelling Strategy

Developing a good fueling strategy – or planning what to eat, and how often – is key to your performance in a stage race.

The first thing to note is that everyone is different – people have different tastes, digestive abilities and preferences. Some runners will fuel a run with a high sugar gel every 40 minutes without missing a beat, others will go all day on the banana they chomped down at the start line.

Experimenting during training and finding what suits you is essential.

Eating when running is hard. Especially when you've been running far, and when it's hot outside – suddenly, that Clif bar is like a leaden block in your hand, and no amount of chewing is going to make it go down.

I generally recommend having some type of fuel every hour – be it a gel or a handful of nuts. Elite ultra-runners survive on one gel every 30-40 minutes for the duration of the event, while many other distance runners will only eat every 3-4 hours on the trail, or when they feel hungry.

Having a strategy and sticking to it is important – this way you will be constantly fueling your body at the rate you are comfortable with.

"If you find you can't stomach bars or gels during your run, attempt a **high calorie carbohydrate drink**. *If you fill it up every 10km you can get upwards of 200-300 calories every rest station."*
- **Brendan Funk, 4 Deserts Grand Slammer**

Gels

These syrupy sweet wonderpacks are specifically designed for athletic performance, delivering instant energy to your body. They typically are a mix of maltodextrin and fructose (plus added flavours) both of which can be processed quickly into fuel.

Most gel users would take them for an event of two hours or more. They typically give you a 100 calorie, 40 minute energy boost, so most manufacturers recommend taking one every 40 minutes – that is, if you can stomach their sticky sweetness!

That's one of the main drawbacks of gels – they taste like a synthetically sweetened honey. If you can get past that, they can be an ideal fuel form. Some people always need a drink with them to wash down the gels.

Some gels have added caffeine – this can be your friend in long runs, but trial them before using them on a race.

Also, some gels are more watery than others (high5 for example), which help you swallow them.

Snacks (Trail Mix, Nuts, Crisps, Etc.)

Salty, tasty snacks such as salted nuts and salami sticks have about the highest calorie per gram ratio of anything out there – and they tend to be exactly what your body craves a few hours into a run!

Crushing up pretzels and chips are a great way to make them fit into a smaller space, and easier to eat while running too. I recommend filling a zip-lock with your salty snacks of choice, then eating handfuls throughout your run, alternating between gels and whatever else you have available.

Other foods recommended to me by runners while researching this book include:

Instant mashed potatoes, Parmeasan cheese (heaven in a stage race - but greasy, requires a dedicated ziplock bag), popcorn kernels (make them with oil in your titanium cup), salami sticks, bananas, sweet potatoes, peanut butter sandwiches. . .

The list goes on when it comes to race snacks. The trick is to find what works for you, and learn what you can stomach when you've been out on the trails for hours on end. You don't want to eat a banana from an aid station halfway through the race, only to discover it doesn't agree with your guts. So, when selecting your race food, remember – high calorie content, palatable and easy to eat!

Food After You Run

As soon as you finish running each stage you should be thinking about recovery. Hopefully when you get to the finish line you'll find you've developed a healthy appetite anyway. Eating something with protein in it is important to let your body get to work on the muscles you've been working out all day.

Protein Powder

Many sports nutrition companies sell lightweight, single-serving sachets of powdered protein – these are slim and practical enough to take in your pack. After you've crossed the finish line, grab a bottle of water and mix one of these in – sip it as you sit with your feet elevated – and your body will thank you for kick-starting the recovery process.

Dehydrated Meals

Protein powder is a good start, but you really want to start replenishing your whole body with real food as soon as you are able to. Eating something within the first hour of crossing the finish line is recommended for getting your system back on track.

The evening time, when you've finished running and your body has relaxed a little, is normally the best opportunity to load up on calories. Dehydrated meals are by far the most common means of replacing those calories on stage races, and while some runners still baulk at them, the wide range of dishes available means that almost everybody can find a meal-in-a-bag that suits them.

Companies such as Mountain House and Expedition Foods sell meals in 200g packs, typically serving 800 calories each.

Many runners find the dehydrated meals to be bland on their own so add salt, pepper or spices. And a word of advice is to take a different meal for each day – if it turns out on day 1 you can't stand the Mac and Cheese, you don't want to have another five packs of it sitting in your bag for the rest of the week!

Instant noodles are another popular option - they are super lightweight, tasty and fulfilling.

Condiments, such as the salt and pepper sachets from restaurants, can make those dehydrated meals taste a little bit more interesting, and help replace sodium levels as you recover.

Hydration

Keeping yourself hydrated is important during long runs, but that doesn't mean you should just drink as much water as you can. Drinking too much can lead to stomach slosh, or – much worse – hyponatremia, if you completely mess up your salt balance.

Likewise, dehydration during a run can lead to medical issues, and certainly doesn't do your kidneys any good.

It's been often quoted recently that many more people have died of over-hydration than dehydration during athletic events. With this in mind, the current medical advice for performing activities where you sweat a lot is **to just drink when you begin to feel thirsty**. This has also been described as 'drinking a sufficient amount to prevent thirst'.

Regarding consumption rates, 500ml/hr is regarded as a minimum amount. Typically in a distance running event, each aid station will offer 1.5l of water – the average runner will find this to be an adequate amount over 10km in hot conditions – many people find this to be excessive.

In regular conditions, your body can process 700-750ml of water per hour - that's the absorption rate through the GI tract. In extreme heat, like in a race, this might increase slightly. But bear this in mind - if you drink over a litre of water an hour, your body can't process it all at once, so it's going to end up sloshing around somewhere (your stomach).

Personally, I find that using a bottle with a straw-like sipper makes staying hydrated very easy. I take tiny sips of water all the time, and find this is an effective way of balancing my hydration. You can practice for this by sipping setting an alarm on your watch to sound every 5 minutes as you run, reminding you to sip

As with every aspect of distance running, the trick with keeping your hydration balanced is in the training – experiment with different quantities when you go for a run, and find out what suits you. Water should be consumed gradually and continuously over a run, in small sips rather than large volumes.

Salts

Humans are salty animals – our blood has the same salinity as seawater. When we run long distances, we sweat – and replace the sweat with fresh, clean water. The problem is, we lose a lot of salt through our sweat, so we've got to look at ways of replacing the salt too.

Hyponatremia

Ultra-runners have ended up in comas from drinking too much water and not replacing their salts – this condition is known as hyponatremia. The sudden dilution of your system and lack of minerals throws your body into a tailspin, leading to disorientation – then it can escalate quickly from there. Don't worry too much about hyponatremia - as long as you are conscious of your salt and hydration levels, it's extremely unlikely you'll have any issues.

How to take salts

The simplest way to replenish your body's salt level is with salt capsules – tiny dissolvable pills that are pure salt. Easy to swallow, compact and handy.

Another option is effervescent tablets such as the 'Nuun' brand – drop one of these in your water bottle and it fizzes up, mixing your required salts in with your water supply. They come in different flavours and some have added minerals, and caffeine, in with them. It is worth remembering that when these fizz up, the bubbles and froth can start to drip out of the sipper on your water bottle. Their synthetic taste isn't for everyone, and will remain in your water bottle long after you've cleaned them out.

When to take salt? The simplest way to take your salts is at every check point, assuming there is one roughly every 10km. That way, you take the salts at the same time you fill up your water supply, and are less likely to forget about them.

How much to take? There's little science here, and trying to calculate how much salt you lose in sweat and how much you need to replace that can get you in knots – I tend to err on the side of 'too much salt is better than not enough', so usually stick to 1 or 2 salt capsules at every 10km check point. If you are a very slow walker in hot conditions then consider taking more between aid stations.

RACER PROFILE: TONY BRAMMER

Tony set out to complete a single 4 Deserts race back in 2005, then went on to complete each of the races in the series - joining the 4 Deserts Club in 2008.

Since then, he has retired from running stage races but his love for the series has kept him busy Tony is a management volunteer at 4 Deserts and assumes the role of Checkpoint Captain in their races! He even takes his wife, son and daughter along these days, and they make regular appearances at checkpoints in various deserts round the world. Having been involved with 22 stage races at time of writing, Tony has a unique perspective - having run the races himself, he has gone on to support thousands of runners in completing stage races.

Hi Tony, what was the first thing that attracted you to stage races?

It started as a mid-life crisis thing, I was looking for a complete mental and physical challenge, I wanted to know how tough I was. I sent Mary Gadams and e-mail and before I knew it I had signed up for the first 4 Deserts Sahara Race in 2005. I wasn't very tough, I cried every day, I hated every step of the race and swore I would never do another race. I hate camping, I hate sleeping in a sleeping bag, I was a really shit competitor. I was just very lucky.

How did you go from a competitor at a single event to a management volunteer, essentially dedicating a huge chunk of your free time to these races?

I had completed a couple of my 4 Deserts races with a new found friend, John Barrett, a Canadian with a Manc sense of humour. John had not completed the Sahara Race and we were both going to Antarctica in 2008 when John had completed the Sahara in October. I suggested that I would register as a volunteer so we could say we had done all four together. I volunteered and I was hooked. I morphed from volunteer, to looking after a CP to being the first Checkpoint Captain to helping with the training to running the training to managing the volunteers. I love what I do and the people I work with and I can't imagine a time when I won't be doing it.

These races are all very memorable, but are there any particular unforgettable moments you can share?

Any night looking up at the stars in the Atacama, listening to the camp team sing in Namibia, crying with laughter in the management meetings at midnight, every time I get to a race and meet up with old friends, and more recently watching my three adopted desert daughters, Cindy Drinnan, Rhianon

West and Tayla Ridley all complete the Patagonia race, a very proud moment.

How do stage races influence other aspects of your life, whether personal or professional?

I have been lucky to witness the complete human spirit, sadly for me it has made me less tolerant of the whingers and moaners in "normal" life, I find people quite disappointing and spend most of the time saying "what is wrong with people?"

What advice would you give to someone preparing for their first ever stage race?

Do the little things well, read the rules, fill your forms out, sort your travel out, get your pack weight below 10kg, train like you intend to race and learn how to pack your bag, run when you can, walk when you can't and cry the rest of the time. Make sure you have plenty of money because it's very addictive and your first race won't be your last. If you are mid pack and below, don't kid yourself it's a mental battle, it's not, it's a huge physical challenge and if you haven't trained hard no amount of mental toughness will get you through.

What are some of the common errors you see runners making when you meet them at race registration / equipment check?

You would swear blind that we never sent them a list of equipment, it's like we asked them to bring some kit and them secretly checked it against a random list. The top competitors don't get it wrong, they don't want a penalty. Whistles on bags, red flashing lights, compression bandages and please don't get me started about patches on rain jackets. We once had a guy bring a pair of compasses as well as a compass, in fairness English wasn't his first language and I guess if the equipment list was in his language I would make more mistakes than him. The equipment should be a gimme, it really isn't that difficult.

When someone comes into a checkpoint, tired, sweating and clearly having a bad day, how do you handle them? How do you assess their state, and reassure them?

I'm usually at the last checkpoint before camp so I suggest that stopping here is not a good idea and they should really get to camp and consider their options. I would say, "while you're sitting here the finish line isn't getting any closer". As long as they are medically capable and we can support them I would encourage them go on, you don't want to go home and wonder if you could have done it. I have a huge amount of empathy with the people at the back of the race, their accomplishment is never diminished by their position, they all get the same medal.

Ryan Sandes in his acceptance speech at the Atacama Crossing 2010 said how he admired the people at the back, out there all day in that heat, he stated "I couldn't do that" and some wag shouted, "why don't you fucking try" touché.

7. RACE PREPARATION

When it comes to stage races, there is a lot more to preparation than simply doing your running training and buying all your equipment on the internet.

When entering a race that lasts several days, the stakes are much higher. If you screw something up - whether it's your travel plans, your pack weight or your documentation - it can ruin an entire week and/or international journey.

This section looks at:

- When and how to buy and test your equipment

- Pre-race footcare

- Making travel plans

- Administrative stuff

- Contingency planning.

Equipment Preparation

As soon as you commit to your stage race you should be thinking about equipment. Ideally, this is 6+ months prior to the race - plenty of time to buy and try every piece of gear, and incorporate it into your training.

The first thing I typically do is establish an equipment list in the form of an Excel spreadsheet. You can use the checklists I've included in the Appendices in this book, or download my Excel-based examples at www.marathonhandbook.com and click on the Stage Races section.

Get the race organiser's mandatory equipment list, and consider every optional piece of equipment you might want to take - then populate your equipment list accordingly. From here, you know what you need to buy.

Where to buy stage race equipment? A lot of the equipment is fairly niche - while you can usually find backpacks and sleeping bags in most town centre shops, they won't be optimised for stage races. They'll be too bulky or heavy or not designed for the rigors of a week of running. Same goes for the food - you need to seek out food that has been specifically designed to maximise calories while minimising weight. So, you either have to find a good outdoors store or head online. Most stage race organisers will have recommended retailers - if they don't have their own online store.

Testing Equipment

It's important to test all your race gear well in advance of your stage race - a slight chafe can turn into a festering open wound over a 250km event. I like to test each piece of gear as early as possible. Areas to focus on include:

- The backpack. Obviously, it's very important to have a backpack which fits you well. When you test it, you should try and fill it with the same equipment and food you are going to bring on the stage race, in order to simulate the actual race conditions. If you don't have all the equipment yet, I can recommend bags of pasta to fill the backpack - they are roughly the same density as the equipment and food you'll bring along. I've learned from experience that bags of rice are too dense, so sit too low in your pack. When testing your backpack, pay attention to the position and tightness of chest and waist straps, and how comfortable the pack is against your back.

- Hydration systems. You should test your hydration system with it full of water, to ensure you can move comfortably without it bouncing around everywhere. You also want to check its practicality - how easy is it to get a sip of water, how easy will it be to re-fill, etc.

- Shoes and socks combo. By the time your event comes around, you want to have absolute faith that the shoes/socks you have chosen will do the job for you.

- Gaiters (optional). Test the gaiters to ensure that they fasten securely to your running shoes, and don't let sand in. Don't wait until you're in the desert to learn that they don't fasten well.

Dress Rehearsal

At least once before your race, it's well worth taking the time to go out and do a medium to long training run in all the gear you intend to wear during the actual event. I call this the 'dress rehearsal'. You should schedule this for 4-6 weeks before your race to allow time for changing anything. This 'dry run' will identify any kinks in your approach before the big race.

- Wear every piece of gear you plan to run with. This means hat, sunglasses, shirt, hydration system, gaiters. The idea is to mimic the conditions of your actual race as best you can.

- If you are planning to tape or lubricate your feet before the race, do the same on your dress rehearsal.

- Food, hydration and salts. Whatever your hydration/salt/gel/snack programme is, now is the time to trial it. Get used to using your watch to fuel and hydrate on a regular basis.

- Accessibility. Does your pack have a few small pockets you can access while running? Good. Decide now what you will keep in each one - things like snacks, gels, salts - as well as a basic toilet kit (paper, hand sanitiser) - camera, buff, iPod?

Body Weight

Your body weight can have a big effect on your stage race performance, so it's always worth considering it during your training. It's not unusual for racers (especially in self-supported stage races) to spend a lot of money on ultra-light gear to shave off a few hundred grams, then turn up at the start line a few kilos over their 'fighting weight'. Whether it's in your backpack or on your hips, excess weight is excess weight – and makes the race that much harder.

In the weeks leading up to your stage race, it is worth looking at ways of making yourself leaner. I'm not recommending that you starve yourself, but by cutting out things like cheese and alcohol, you can easily lose a few of the extra pounds that you've been carrying around. It all makes a difference on the race.

Pre-Race Footcare

It is worth spending some time on your feet in the two months prior to the race. The best way to take care of your feet is with good shoes and socks, but there are several steps you can take prior to your race to further minimise the chances of problems:

Toenails should be trimmed back, as a minimum, to ensure there's no rubbing as you run. Many runners file their toenails too - the idea is to remove any sharp edges, which can easily catch on sock material and rub. Ingrown toenails are very common on distance runners, so checking for these is important too.

As a distance runner, it's easy to build up areas of thick skin and callouses in various areas of your soles. This happens naturally over time, but can lead to blisters - and if a blister occurs under a section of thick skin, it is much harder to treat. Prior to a race, I use a pumice stone to work away any areas of my feet that feel too thick and old. However, remember that thick skin has built up for a reason - to protect - so don't take it all off and leave your foot completely pink and bare! Only remove areas that seem excessively thick and could be problematic.

As odd as it may sound, many runners go for a pedicure prior to stage races. They'll take care of your toenails and areas of thick skin, and generally make your feet feel great! Watch out however - if the masseuse doesn't realise you're a distance runner, they might try and sand down all that well-developed extra thickness that you've developed.

Race Documentation

This is another area you want to address as soon as you practically can. The race organisers typically ask for a signed disclaimer as well as a doctor's line declaring that you are capable of completing the race.

It is worthwhile to take plenty of time to study all the available race details too - such as the rules, the course description, FAQs, route map, etc.

Travel Planning Essentials

Book Early

As soon as you've committed to your stage race, you should look at travel plans. Especially when it comes to far-flung locations, the earlier you can book things the better, in terms of price and availability.

This is especially pertinent if a race is in a remote location - 300 runners descending on a small town often means that every flight / taxi / hotel fills up quickly, so the faster you can get things in place the better.

Get Travel Insurance

There are two types of insurance you should consider when you're booking a big running-based trip: cancellation, and health. Cancellation is in case the organisers pull the event for some reason - you can recoup any expenses made on travel arrangements.

Health insurance is more specialised - it's unlikely that any existing travel insurance you have covers stage races. Most 'extreme sports' are in the 'exempt' list of the big policy providers, which means you have to seek out a special insurance policy for the week of your trip. Some providers which cover ultra-marathons include: Dog Tag, The British Mountaineering Council and Harrison Beaumont. Before buying your policy check the terms and conditions of your chosen provider against the race organiser's rules about (for example) deposits and cancellations to make sure you're properly covered.

Travel Documentation

Visas – these may be required if you are travelling overseas for your race. The race organiser should be able to advise you on visa requirements, but it's not a bad idea to double-check these yourself. Every country has different visa policies, and these change depending on your own nationality, but these days most countries have a simple online application, or visa-on-arrival system. Depending on your destination, the airline will check your visa when you check-in: no visa, no plane ticket.

Proof of onward travel – this is something a lot of airlines, and customs officers, are sticklers for. Basically, they want to see a piece of paper showing you've got plans to leave the country you are racing in. Assuming you've booked a return ticket, this is your 'proof' – if you've got more complex travel plans, make sure you're prepared to present them / explain yourself when quizzed.

Required inoculations – a few countries require these – some African countries require proof of a yellow fever inoculation, for example. Your race organiser should advise you on these. However, it never hurts to do a quick Google search, just in case.

Address while in the country – the immigration officer might ask you for this when you arrive, so make sure you've got the name of the hotel you're going to at hand – even if you're only staying there for one night.

What If My Luggage Gets Lost?

A nightmare scenario – you arrive at your final destination, deep in the jungle, but your suitcase with all your race gear is lost somewhere else. It's an unlikely situation, but one that happens to some poor soul on almost every race, so worth spending a few minutes preparing for it by considering the following two questions:

1: "What pieces of equipment are absolutely mandatory, i.e. you couldn't start the race without?"

These items, as much as humanly possible, should be packed in your hand luggage. Think shoes, race pack, running clothes, sleeping bag, and anything else you can cram in.

2: "What items could be replaced once I get to the host town, if they go missing?"

No matter how remote you find yourself, chances are there's a stall selling instant noodles, crisps, salted nuts and sugary supplies – a.k.a. a "Race Nutrition Supply Store". Despite the high prices we pay for our specialised, dehydrated meals, in actual fact we are surprisingly well catered-for in most locales. So unless you have very specific nutritional requirements, you should be fine to put most of your race food in with your luggage.

RACER PROFILE: FILIPPO ROSSI

Filippo Rossi has run both Marathon des Sables and every race in the 4 Deserts series – in fact, in 2016 he completed the 4 Deserts Grand Slam, consistently achieving top-10 positions.

A seasoned ultrarunner whose pack is always lighter than everyone else's', Filippo knows how to run far.

What was it about the 4 Deserts races that first caught your eye?

When I first came to Namibia, I already had the MDS experience behind me. I was confident about what was going on. However, the environment of people was completely different. This is what stunned me at first. The idea to meet worldwide people much more deeper than what I had experienced before. In terms of racing, of course I saw a difference in the organization. Even though 4 Deserts was always very well organized, they missed some facilities that MDS provided automatically.

How did your preparation for stage races evolve, from one race to the next?

I must say that after MdS I changed completely the vision of training because I changed my trainer. That happened just before my first 4 Deserts race in Namibia. Since then I radically improved my running style and my consciousness about it, making it possible to train and know what I was doing. During the Grand Slam then, I continued improving this consciousness that today allows me to train much more efficiently.

What was the biggest challenges, or scary moments, of the 4 Desert Grand Slam?

The challenges were everywhere. Time to recover was never enough. Races were tough and no discount has been made, even for the grand slammers. The biggest challenge was mentally. Keeping the mind set ready for the next challenge. When I finished Antarctica, I was scared of what was coming next, because I entered a loop. The scariest moment was during the Atacama Crossing, when I really considered the dropping out because of a stomach acidity problem, which I solved just by downing some pills that the doctor gave me.

However, the problems still persisted and I finished the run with a lot of problems, compromising the result.

Can you share what your pack weights were, and how you managed to reduce them so much??

This is maybe the funniest thing you have to do before going to the desert. Preparing the backpack is an art. I started at MDS with more than 8kgs and finished this year at the Iranian Silk Road Ultramarathon with just 6.5kg. Not bad. But how? Simply getting rid of anything that isn't useful for the race. The food is really tight and minimal for the whole week, which means that you get the calories you need from a very small amount of food. Then all the small items like knife, lamps and mirrors are really basic, as the sleeping bag, which is no more than 300g. Considering all the mandatory equipment that RTP requires, which is far too much, I was always able to keep the weight low without cheating.

How do stage races influence other aspects of your life, whether personal or professional?

Stage races changed my life.

I must say that after journalism, my profession, I live for running. I would love to run any kind of stage races in the world if I just had the time. You live such intense experiences and meet such amazing people that it really touches you. Personally, it helped me a lot, being stronger mentally and much more consecutive. Professionally also, since my work brings me to risk anytime, I always need concentration and determination, which is also thanks to these races.

Did you get any bad injuries during the 4 Deserts Grand Slam?

Fortunately not, I finished Antarctica just with bad tendons inflammations, but that was fair enough considering the terrain and the hardness of the course.

What was it like running 250km in Antarctica?

Antarctica was surely an awesome experience that I would maybe repeat without racing such a race. 250km run on a loop-range that goes from 1.5km to 3.5km for 10 hours, is far too much, even for the strongest. This proves you mentally and physically, since you're never on a hard path, the weather changes every minute and the loops are so tiny that you always have to pass people making double efforts. I considered that race as a proof for my head, and the result was perfect since I came 3rd out of 60 people. Talking about the fact of running in Antarctica, that was priceless. Animals and landscapes were just something unexplainable and I will never forget it.

What advice would you give to someone preparing for their first ever stage race?

The best advice I can give is doing like me: find someone that already did it and let him guide you, especially for the gear. The most important thing is the gear and the food. Logistics make more than half of everything.

Training and mental are important too, but if you go with a wrong pair of shoes or you bring the wrong food (which is always my case, after 6 times), you will not finish or you will just hate the experience. This is what I did: I got to know a guy, who is one of my best friends today, that already did MdS. I asked him, learnt from him. He finally checked my equipment and told me if I was missing something. Done. My MdS was a success.

Any 'secret sauce' tips / quirky things you do to help you during stage races?

For sure anyone develops his own strategies. For me, for example, comfort is everything. I learnt that gaiters are not always useful. If you don't have dunes, you don't need them. Salt tablets are essential as the electrolytes are. I personally take only tablets, avoiding taking liquids that could disturb your stomach with predictable bad-turnings. Eventually I would add the shorts. Tights with more pockets are good to bring more energy bars, salts and everything you need during the race without always opening the bags, stopping and losing time and rhythm. It is simple: just take any kind of tights and tell a tailor to sew some elastic pockets (tailor-made). This is a winning strategy if you also want to avoid the front pack.

8. THE STAGE RACE

It is finally time for the race itself.

In an ideal world, your stage race would be a reflection of your hard work you did during your training and preparation. After all those months of sweating and planning, your body is in perfect condition and the race is a smooth and enjoyable experience from start to finish.

The problem with stage races is that this very rarely happens. Part of any stage race is accepting Murphy's Law - whatever can happen, will happen. If you can anticipate this and be prepared for the bumps along the road, you'll be able to weather them much better.

Daily Routine

It's worth having a rough routine to stick to when you are on a stage race - with so much to remember it's easy to overlook something. Here's an example:

Pre-race:

- 90 minutes before race start - alarm to wake up, get dressed into running clothes inside sleeping bag. Get up, use bathroom and have breakfast.

- 60 minutes before race start - brush teeth, pack all equipment into backpack.

- 30 minutes before race start - dress feet (blisters, tape, socks, lubricant), put on running shoes.

- 20 minutes before race start - sweep tent to ensure everything is clear. Check backpack is good to go. Prepare gels and snacks in accessible pockets.

- 10 minutes before race start - use bathroom again, fill up on water, last minute checks

Post-race:

- Get water, if required.

- Go to tent and set down backpack.

- Remove socks and shoes, find a good spot to lie down with feet elevated.
- Elevate feet for min. 30 minutes, drink protein shake to re-hydrate / recover.

- Eat a snack.

- Get any blisters / feet issues addressed.

- Eat evening meal after you have relaxed.

Footcare During a Stage Race

No matter how well you've prepared and conditioned your feet prior to your run, you can't predict what's going to happen when you're out on the trails. During stage races, the majority of competitors have foot issues that require treatment at some point.

I've provided some brief advice below, but recommend anyone that's serious about footcare during races studies *'Fixing Your Feet'* by John Vonhof – it's the bible on all things feet, and is written with ultra-running and multi-stage events in mind.

Hot Spots

These are your first indication that something is up – a feeling of irritation coming from somewhere on your feet that doesn't go away. When you feel a hot spot and recognise that it's not going to disappear, it's best to stop and check things out. Running through a hot spot will almost always make things worse.

It may just be caused by a bunched-up sock or some sand, and can easily be remedied in less than a minute. Or it may be the start of a bigger problem, like rubbing - which will lead to blisters.

Blisters

To pot or not to pop? Generally, if a blister forms during a long race, it's unlikely to go away so it's best dealt with earlier rather than later. I always recommend checking with the medical crew if they are available, but here's the rough guide to doing it yourself:

1. Clean the area around the blister.

2. Pop it with a sterilised needle around the sides – making 3 or 4 tiny holes around the blister helps keep it drained.

3. Clean and dry the blister – do not remove any of the loose skin!

4. Dress the blister with Elastikon / sticky dressing tape. The application style will depend on where your blister is, but generally you want to ensure the tape is applied completely flush with your foot (no folds), and is positioned to hold on. For example, if the blister occurs on the arch of your foot, wrap the tape around the bottom of your foot so there is a bit of grip – last thing you want is the tape to come off and have to re-dress the blister later.

Foot Maceration

Some people call this trench foot – it's basically when the skin of your feet is saturated in water. Imagine what your feet look like after half an hour in a hot bath and you're in the right ballpark – picture running an ultra on those. They are much more susceptible to blisters and wounds. Many runners who train in cold, dry climates experience foot maceration when they run in hot, humid countries – or when their feet get wet.

The best way to prevent foot maceration is to keep your feet dry. First and foremost, this means aiming for wicking socks and breathable shoes – i.e. footwear that drains and doesn't hold water easily. Secondly, it means avoiding water crossings if possible – and if you can't avoid them, assessing whether a change of socks would be prudent when you come out the other side. Thirdly, and hopefully unnecessary, is using products such as gels and powders that keep your feet dry (such as talcum powder).

And what to do if you suffer from foot maceration? The number one cure is to let your feet dry out – hopefully you've made it to the end of the day with your feet still holding up, so whip off your socks and air out your soles. Hopefully you've got some dry gear to throw on in the morning. A dry dressing may go some way to pulling some of the moisture out and providing some cushioning for when you have to get back to the trails.

Tips from The Trails

Here is some of the best advice I've collected on how to tackle stage races, whether mentally or physically:

Take It Checkpoint to Checkpoint

A 42km, 50km or 100km race is often too big and daunting a single task to fully comprehend when you're in the middle of it. When it comes to week-long stage races, thinking about your progress in terms of a whole week can be overwhelming, and counterproductive - especially in the early stages.

Once you're out on the trail, it can seem overwhelming to try and calculate just how much distance you've still got to run. Instead, a popular approach is to only focus on the next checkpoint. Typically, checkpoints are around 10 km apart – so this breaks the race down into manageable chunks, rather than one mammoth undertaking. Only focusing on getting to the next checkpoint is the easiest way to 'trick' your brain into pushing on when the going is getting tough.

Have a Checkpoint Strategy

Have a plan for what you are going to do at checkpoints before you even start the race. Are you planning to just fill up on water and keep moving, or do you intend to factor in rest stops? My normal approach is to never sit down, unless I really need to – if you sit down when you're tired, it's so much harder to get back up.

Having said that, checkpoints provide a great opportunity to take stock and make sure you're really doing alright. If you have stones or sand in your shoes, now is a good time to take them out.

In extreme conditions of heat and humidity, some people find it prudent to factor in 5-10 minute 'refreshment' stops at the checkpoints. Swollen fingers and hands can be common in hot environments, so at the checkpoint stand around with your hands above your head for five minutes in the shade.

Some people really do savour the checkpoints and enjoy the company and ambience - this is personal preference. I try and push on and continue running if I am feeling capable, so I can relax when I reach the finish point for each day.

Walking

The biggest myth surrounding stage races and ultra-running in general is that the majority of people run the entire event - the truth is, almost no-one does. In fact, you can walk the whole way and still do well.

Over the course of a long race, you'll see the 'tortoise and hare' effect play out several times: a steady walker beating the shuffling runner. This is usually because the runner expends a high amount of energy in their shuffle, so has to stop and rest for 20 minutes at every checkpoint. On a typical multi-stage race such as a 4 Deserts event, a comfortable, consistent walker will typically finish around the middle of the pack.

For this reason, you might want to plan a rough run/walk schedule. It can be especially helpful towards the end of a stage, where your energy is sagging. Run for 5 minutes, walk for 2 minutes - or similar. On one exceptionally hot day in a race in Cambodia, I stuck in my iPod and would alternate between running and walking every time a new song started.

Pace

At the finish line of a race, look for the runners who look happy, relaxed and have done well – chances are, these are the people who have run a fairly consistent pace. The same principle applies in stage races, but is compounded. Go out too fast on day one, and you'll suffer for it on the remaining five stages. Choose a pace which is going to get you round the course in a good time, but will leave some energy in the tank for the next day.

Find a Buddy

The benefits of running, or walking, with a friend shouldn't be underestimated. When the trails get tough, the last thing you want is to turn around and see no other runners. Passing the time with other runners can help take your mind off any discomforts you have and make the day pass quicker. On especially tough days it's pretty common for runners to wait at a checkpoint for the next runner behind them to catch up, so they can continue together. Plus, running together with someone is a great way to share the experience and get to know another runner. And for the racers, running near others is a great way to keep your own pace up!

Running with Music

Studies have proven that listening to music while running can improve your performance. It really comes down to personal preference, but many people find that music can really help you push through the latter stages of an ultra-marathon. I typically use either my iPhone (doubles up as a camera) or an iPod shuffle (weighs less than 20g and lasts for 12hrs+), and will save my music for the latter stages of the race when I need something to give me a boost.

Getting Lost

Most stage race courses are marked with tape and markers, roughly every 30 ft or so. Although they are easy to follow, you'd be surprised how often runners 'tune out' and miss a turn or go down the wrong path.

If you find yourself lost, go back to the last course marker and try and find your way from there. If there is no clear route in sight, then your next move is to either wait for another runner to arrive, or back-track to the last checkpoint.

While backtracking is nobody's favourite game, it beats being lost – and chances are, if you can't find the next marker, nobody else will be able to either. If you're truly lost, hopefully you've got a mobile phone, or as a minimum the contact details of the support staff.

Finish Day Two

If you look at the attrition rate (dropout rate) of a six-stage event, you'll see a clear trend in every single race: the rate of drop-outs decreases as the event goes on.

This is mainly down to two reasons:

1. the first couple of days weeds out anybody who is under-prepared or under-committed

2. people get more determined to finish as they get closer to the finish line.

The first couple of days of a multi-stage are always taxing – exotic environments, sleeping outdoors, physical exertion, different food – however, you'd be surprised how your body adapts to these conditions and by the end of the week it seems 'normal'.

With this in mind, I think that the end of day 2 is a great 'line in the sand' – if you've made it to the end of day 2, then your odds of finishing have just skyrocketed. After day 2 is completed, you just have to complete day 3 and you are half-way finished. Once you're past half-way, everything is easier!

Get Yourself to The Start Line of The Next Stage

"Many runners will say you feel absolutely knackered after day one and have no idea how you will start again the next morning for day two. After stage one on my first KAEM (2013) I was about to pull the pin…. chances are that you will feel pretty good the next morning.

Never drop out at the end of a stage unless recommended by the medics.

Never drop out at the beginning of a stage unless recommended by the medics."

- **Peter Jorgensen,** stage race veteran

Tired, injured, mentally exhausted – so many runners walk into a campsite at the end of a tough stage and are so defeated they just pull the plug on the whole race then and there.

Worst idea ever.

Dropping out after completing a stage without a good medical reason is a decision that will nag at you for months or years afterwards – probably until you go back and do the race again. I've met several runners who would put themselves into this group.

If you've had a rough day on the trail but make it back to camp in one piece, you owe it to yourself to get some rest, then at least drag yourself to the start line of the next day. The worst possible scenario then becomes that you start off and can't keep going, so drop out at CP1. But if you can make it to CP1, then you can probably make it to CP2…then it's just a matter of taking it a checkpoint at a time.

"It may not be medically advisable, but you can work through a lot more than you think. During my first stage race in Namibia I was unable to eat anything solid for 2 days. Despite this, I was able to get down somewhere around 1,000 calories a day via drink mixes. This didn't do any favors for my bowels, but it got me through the toughest part of the race in one piece. The point is to be creative with your food. Maybe your plan goes awry, that is ok. If you are prepared enough, you can still make it through."

- **Brendan Funk, 4 Deserts Grand Slammer**

The Art of the DNF

D.N.F. = Did Not Finish.

This is what gets written next to your name on the results sheet if you drop out - that is, if you fail to complete the race, for whatever reason.

Stage races by their nature have a high dropout rate - typically 10-25% of the people who start a stage race don't finish.

People drop out for a variety of reasons, and anything can happen during a 5 or 6 stage race - it's not just the underprepared who encounter issues. Heat exhaustion, injury, health issues - these crop up a lot.

If you find yourself unable to continue or are told by the staff that your race is over, it can be a crushing experience. You've trained so much and committed so much time and effort to your preparation. Yet it happens so often to well-prepared runners.

Often runners who DNF have three options - stay with the race and work with the support team, return to the host town/hotel, or go home. Going home might not be an option if you're in an international race and your flights are all booked up already. So, I **would generally advocate considering staying at the race and supporting it**. You are still able to experience the race in some capacity, and get to lend support to your friends and fellow runners. The alternative is to go and relax in a hotel, and enjoy the huge feeling of missing out on something cool.

Another fact is that a runner who DNF's often becomes even more determined, and swears to return and complete the race in following year. For many, their stage race becomes a personal battle - something they have to overcome - so a DNF is not the end of the story. In fact, it can compel you to double-down and return the following year stronger and better prepared.

To me, the best way to approach a DNF is all in your preparation.

Remind yourself that there's an inherent risk of DNF, no matter how good a runner you are. Assume that you may have to pull out at some point, and picture what it might look like if this happens.

Before I even start running a race, I am considering what a DNF might look like. I chat with the support crew and picture myself working with them - this helps make it easier if I do end up dropping out. A few days spent encouraging and supporting your fellow runners is still a great experience!

RACER PROFILE: DION LEONARD

(Photo credit: WAA Ultra)

Dion Leonard is an extreme runner and stage race veteran, having tackled the Marathon des Sables several times, along with 2 x KAEM (Kalahari Augrabies Extreme Marathon), MdS Peru, the 4 Deserts 'Gobi March' race and Global Limits Cambodia to name a few – regularly bagging podium spots for his troubles.

Dion lives with his wife, Lucja – also an extreme runner – in Edinburgh, Scotland. He became an international figure in

2016 when he befriended a stray dog whilst running across the Chinese Gobi Desert, and went on to adopt the dog – named Gobi. He recounted the story in the International bestseller 'Finding Gobi'. Follow Dion's running adventures on twitter @findinggobi.

Hi Dion, you've run a lot of stage races but are especially known for your affinity to the Marathon des Sables. What was it about the MdS that first appealed to you?

MDS is the iconic blue riband event when it comes to multi stage races. It's the best of the best when it comes to runners, organisation and desert challenges. I remember first watching and being captivated by the beauty of the Sahara Desert and thought to myself one day I would love to experience it.

What mistakes did you make in your first MdS preparation?

I'd completed the Kalahari Augrabies Extreme 250km in the South African Kalahari Desert a few months earlier so was well prepared for running in the heat and sand. What I wasn't prepared for was the sand dunes and the size of them. At my first MDS on Stage 1 we ran 25km in the famous Merzouga dunes and the wheels came off. I only finished the stage because my wife Lucja caught up to me as I was sitting in the dunes contemplating dropping out but she managed to convince me to get to the finish line. It was a massive wake up call, the race continually feels like its punching you in the face and you just have to pick yourself up day after day.

What has been the biggest failure for you, during stage races - and how have you addressed it?

Recently at the inaugural MDS 250km in Peru across the Ica Desert I struggled with illness. I battled every day to finish and every night I battled to make it to the start line, it was a disaster, everything went wrong and it became the longest week of my life. It took me a few days to forget about how my race from a competitive point of view was ruined but to just appreciate the opportunity, beauty of the area and breathe it all in. You have to adjust your goals during the week as things outside of your control happen and dealing with this quickly will help you get to the finish line.

How do stage races influence other aspects of your life, whether personal or professional?

Multi stage races have changed me completely. I've learnt a lot about myself and every time I complete a race I walk away a different person. These races have you spending a lot of time in your own thoughts and whether its work, family or lifestyle I always come back wanting to improve, change or complete something that I haven't done before. You're also in a unique environment for a week with lots of people from all over the world so you get to meet and spend time with people you wouldn't normally. I've met a lot of wonderful people during multi stage races and made some friends for life from all over the world.

Is it hard to find time to train sufficiently for stage races?

I don't know if it's hard to find the time or its harder to find the motivation. Training is a huge piece of a multi stage race and when it's cold outside but you still need to get that run in then it can be difficult to get out the door. I tend to train a lot more flexibly these days and don't stick to any generic plans. I combine running with cross training, turbo training, indoor rowing and swimming and that keeps things fresh for me.

What advice would you give to someone preparing for their first ever stage race?

Don't be overwhelmed. You need to get 3 things right - training, food and kit. It's simple and doesn't need to be expensive, time consuming or difficult. A lot of forums giving advice really cause more confusion than necessary.

Any 'secret sauce' tips / quirky things you do to help you during stage races?

Sometimes the water given to you during multi stage races is sitting at checkpoints in temperatures of up to 50 degrees and is simply undrinkable. To cool it down, place a wet 'Buff' over your water bottles before you put them in their holders and as you run the breeze combined with the wet 'Buff' will chill your bottles. If you're in the campsite then use the drink bottle nozzle to hang them in the air from a tree or your tent to catch the breeze.

9. CONCLUSION

I hope you have found the information in this book useful. Maybe it will just give you a couple of ideas to implement in your stage race preparation, or maybe it has guided you in a deeper way. Either way, hopefully you've found your time spent in this book to be a good investment.

The chapters of the book cover a lot of wide topics, so I thought I'd use this conclusion to hammer home the key points I'd like to make to anyone preparing for a stage race. Here they are:

Preparation is not just about training to run long distances and buying a bunch of expensive gear.

Training is about conditioning your body and mind to be ready for a week-long race - specific to the conditions of your race. For such a huge undertaking, the most foolproof and structured method is to devise a good training plan early on and follow it well. I always recommend adding some gym work to your training schedule.

Equipment preparation means researching every piece of equipment, making informed decisions about what to take and why you need it, and then testing every piece of equipment thoroughly - so you have a high degree of confidence in your kit before you leave home.

Race preparation is all the auxiliary stuff - booking flights, getting doctor's lines, getting your feet ready - it is an area that most runners simply don't spend enough time on.

The final part of preparation, at least for me, is to visualise ahead and imagine what the race is going to be like. I often ask myself 'what would my experience be like if the race was very challenging, or if I got injured in day one?'. Although every stage race is a huge step into the unknown, doing some pre-race visualisation helps you be ready for what may come.

For most of us, the worst-case scenario will be that we have to drop out - the good news is that then we can spend the remainder of the race supporting the other runners and being a part of the race organiser's team.

And that's it. No matter how much and how well you prepare, at the end of the day every stage race will throw new challenges and unexpected scenarios at you. All I can say is, try to weather them well.

- **Thomas Watson, hi@marathonhandbook.com**

BONUS RACER PROFILE: ASH MOKHTARI (ATACAMA ASH)

Ash Mokhtari has run the 4 Deserts Atacama Crossing a record nine years in a row.

A seasoned ultrarunner, Ash enters a few adventure races every year, from the Canadian Death Race to catered races through Northern Spain. But the Atacama is the only race that Ash goes back to – and he goes back every single year.

Ash has now completed the Atacama Crossing race every year for the past 8 years. The organisers of the race even call him 'Ashacama', and presented him with the Spirit Award for the 2016 edition of the race. When not running crazy races, Ash is a dentist in Thunder Bay, Canada.

Hi Ash! What is it about the Atacama Crossing race in particular that has made you return nine times?

The Atacama Crossing was the first ultra stage race that I actually ran which made long-lasting impressions on me in the sense that I realized I could actually run 250 km in a hostile place with 10 kilos on my back and come out alive. I was really a paradigm shifter for me; a rare experience that allows to see everything in a different light and open up doors for one.

We all live our lives according to our collection of experiences and what we perceive of the world around us and our role and capabilities in the world. It is these experiences and perceptions that limit our boundaries. In that first race, I passed through my boundaries and realized how much more I could do. I've imprinted on that moment and I go back every year, reminding myself I could push a little further. Besides, it's become a tradition for me now. It helps me have something to train for and look forward to when I'm at home.

Could you describe some of the highlights of the Atacama Crossing route that make it special for you?

The race starts high up in the Andes in a colourful Arcoiris Valley (rainbow valley) which is at an elevation of 3200 meters high in the valleys. It's called the rainbow valley because of the multiple colours of the mountains around it due to various mineral deposits. The route winds up and down small passes as we descend closer to the Atacama Desert floor, running through small, narrow valleys that had been used by ancient Inca and Pre-Inca traders for millennia.

On the second day we run through a 10km long slot canyon. It's a narrow, deep, scenic canyon cut into the floor of the valley by thousands of years of flooding. Its definitely one of the highlights of the race and provides action shots for the all the runners. There are numerous sand dunes that we either climb or run down. I have to say I always look forward to running down a sand dune that extends all the way from the top of a ridge to a river at the bottom of a valley.

The finish line is in the charming little town of San Pedro de Atacama. It's a touristy hub which is used for many types excursions into the desert or the mountains and volcanoes that surround it.

For one night, we camp by one of the lakes in the desert which are also home to flamingoes and other unlikely birds of the Andes. It's a beautiful place.

And finally, I have to mention the infamous Salt Flats of the Atacama Desert, with their uneven and running-shoe-chewing terrain. They will bring even the most seasoned ultra runner to an eventual walking pace. At places the salt flats alternate between hard-packed salt sheets, razor sharp crystals growing out of the ground or frozen-cauliflower heads that might crumble into a hole with your foot in it.

Ultimately, the people I meet during the race are the highlights of the race. The runners and the volunteers make the whole experience completely unforgettable. Some my best friends are the people I have met in these races and incredibly after just a couple of days of sharing a tent or a few hours – not even, more like minutes – of conversation on the run or around the camp fire have created long-lasting, close friendships.

Having run the Atacama Crossing race so many times, how do you physically prepare for each one?

I start training six months prior to the race. I have a certain mileage in mind and gradually increase that as I get close to the starting date. Also, I live in Canada which is a frozen fridge and so have difficulty with the heat of the Atacama

177

Desert. So I remedy that by spending 30 minutes in the sauna after my runs.

Ideally if you don't live in a hot place, you want to spend two weeks in the desert to allow your body to acclimatize to the heat. The Atacama is a high altitude desert so the body needs three weeks to acclimatize to the altitude as well. This is not possible for most of us unless you're either retired or a pro ultra runner. Cross training is important because you're running in an environment that you can't practice in, and besides, there's the backpack. I'd run with the pack because you want to get used to it and get your blisters and ranches before you hit the desert floor.

You must meet a lot of 'first timers' when you do this race. What kind of advice do you give them?

Obviously training is very important. The more you train the better, but your overall experience might not get easier. Atacama will humble everybody and will not discriminate (laughing). A lot of first time runners of Atacama see the surrounding mountains and volcanos and forget that they are actually running 2-3 km above sea level. This means there's a lot less oxygen and much harder for the body to produce the amount of energy needed to run a marathon in the first day. So pretty much everybody runs at full speed the first day and ends up paying for it for the rest of the race. I'd say pace yourself on the first day, go slower till your pack is a bit lighter.

Don't bring too much stuff. You really have to work on your packing and cut out the non-essential items.

What type of food do you take on your self-supported races?

Everybody uses freeze dried food available from various brands. My favourite is Chili Con Carne from Expedition foods that RTP (Racing The Planet) sells. There's other companies but you might want to try them at home to make sure you can actually eat them. I recommend noodles and soups just in case you get dehydrated or have nausea and can't stomach solids. Hot chocolate and tea. I always brings a couple of bags of chips. They're easier to eat on the run. I don't recommend hot or sweet foods because once it gets hot most runners can't handle the sugar load. Nuts provide a much safer and powerful calorie bang per weight.

Do you spend additional time before or after the race in San Pedro, or in Chile in general?

I usually do. There's a ton of stuff to do once you get to San Pedro. The town has tens of restaurants and amazing food. My favourite is ceviche chichis – basically marinated sea food which Chile has an unlimited source of. Every restaurant in town has its own recipe and usually after the race I restaurant hop and just order ceviche. There are various tour companies that would take the tourist to various archeological and ecological sites in the desert. A lot of people climb the various volcanoes visible from San Pedro. And since we're only 50km from the Bolivian border, a day trip to Bolivian Alto Planico can be arranged.

Other than the Atacama Crossing, what's some of your other top races?

Racing the Planet stage the Atacama Crossing race but also has races in China and Namibia and a roving race which this year is in Patagonia which I'm headed to after Atacama. I ran Grand To Grand in Utah and that was an excellent race. I ran in Cambodia with Global Limits and that was really great experience. Way of the Legends in Northern Spain is a race I would do again. One of my favourite races is the Keys100 which is very scenic as it goes through the Florida Keys. And finally, closer to home, the Canadian Death Race in the Rockies; 125km of complete unpredictable-ness in 24 hours, scaling three mountain peaks and running wild in the forests of Northern Canada.

APPENDIX - EXAMPLE 6 MONTH TRAINING PLAN

Every runner trains and prepares for stage races differently, depending on their underlying fitness and ambitions for the race.

The following training plan is designed for someone of average fitness, that can currently run one hour without stopping.

The goal of the training plan is to prepare the runner for their race, and this training plan is suited for stage races in that it:
- Gradually builds up the weekly 'long runs' to a maximum of 60 km.
- Includes 'back-to-backs' - long runs on both Saturdays and Sundays.
- Is aimed at building up 'time on your feet', as opposed to focusing on speed.

Training plans should be customised for every runner - to this end, you can download the following plan for free in Excel format over at www.marathonhandbook.com .

WEEK	Monday	Tuesday	Wednesday	Thursday	Friday	Saturday	Sunday
1	Rest Day	1hr normal run	1hr cross training	1hr normal run	Rest / Cross Train	Long Slow Run - 10km	1hr normal run
2	Rest Day	1hr normal run	1hr cross training	1hr normal run	Rest / Cross Train	Long Slow Run - 11km	1hr normal run
3	Rest Day	1hr normal run	1hr cross training	1hr normal run	Rest / Cross Train	Long Slow Run - 12km	1hr normal run
4	Rest Day	1hr normal run	1hr cross training	1hr normal run	Rest / Cross Train	Long Slow Run - 13km	1hr normal run
5	Rest Day	1hr normal run	1hr cross training	1hr normal run	Rest / Cross Train	Long Slow Run - 14km	1hr normal run
6	Rest Day	1hr normal run	1hr cross training	1hr normal run	Rest / Cross Train	Long Slow Run - 15km	1hr normal run
7	Rest Day	1hr normal run	1hr cross training	1hr normal run	Rest / Cross Train	Long Slow Run - 17km	1hr normal run
8	Rest Day	1hr normal run	1hr cross training	1hr normal run	Rest / Cross Train	Long Slow Run - 19km	1hr normal run
9	Rest Day	1hr normal run	1hr cross training	1hr normal run	Rest / Cross Train	Long Slow Run - 20km	2hrs normal run

10	Rest Day	1hr normal run	1hr cross training	1hr normal run	Rest / Cross Train	Long Slow Run - 22km	2hrs normal run
11	Rest Day	1hr normal run	1hr cross training	1hr normal run	Rest / Cross Train	Long Slow Run - 24km	2hrs normal run
12	Rest Day	1hr normal run	1hr cross training	1hr normal run	Rest / Cross Train	Long Slow Run - 26km	2hrs normal run
13	Rest Day	1hr normal run	1hr cross training	1hr normal run	Rest / Cross Train	Long Slow Run - 28km	2hrs normal run
14	Rest Day	1hr normal run	1hr cross training	1hr normal run	Rest / Cross Train	Long Slow Run - 30km	2hrs normal run
15	Rest Day	1hr normal run	1hr cross training	1hr normal run	Rest / Cross Train	Long Slow Run - 33km	2hrs normal run
16	Rest Day	1hr normal run	1hr cross training	1hr normal run	Rest / Cross Train	Long Slow Run - 36km	2hrs normal run
17	Rest Day	1hr normal run	1hr cross training	1hr normal run	Rest / Cross Train	Long Slow Run - 39km	2hrs normal run
18	Rest Day	1hr normal run	1hr cross training	1hr normal run	Rest / Cross Train	Long Slow Run - 42km	Long Slow Run - 42km
19	Rest Day	1hr normal run	1hr cross training	1hr normal run	Rest / Cross Train	Long Slow Run - 45km	Long Slow Run - 45km

20	Rest Day	1hr normal run	1hr cross training	1hr normal run	Rest / Cross Train	Long Slow Run - 48km	2hrs normal run
21	Rest Day	1hr normal run	1hr cross training	1hr normal run	Rest / Cross Train	Long Slow Run - 50km	2hrs normal run
22	Rest Day	1hr normal run	1hr cross training	1hr normal run	Rest / Cross Train	Longest Slow Run - 60km	1.5hrs normal run
23	Rest Day	30mins normal run	1hr light cross training	30mins normal run	Rest / Cross Train	Long Slow Run - 40km	1hr normal run
24	Rest Day	30mins normal run	1hr light cross training	30mins normal run	Rest / Cross Train	Long Slow Run - 30km	30mins normal run
25	Rest Day	30mins light run	1hr light cross training	30mins light run	Rest / Cross Train	Long Slow Run - 15km	30mins light run
26	Rest Day	30mins light run	Rest	30mins light run	rest	Easy 3km run	Race Starts

APPENDIX - EXAMPLE EQUIPMENT LIST: SELF-SUPPORTED STAGE RACE

The below equipment and food list includes all the typical equipment a runner might take to a self-supported stage race - it is not race-specific and not necessarily comprehensive. See the Equipment and Race Preparation chapters for much more on this.

How to Use:

- Download the Equipment List below over at marathonhandbook.com in the Stage Race section.
- Check it first against your race's mandatory and optional equipment lists, to make sure it covers everything the race director has told you to take.
- Check it against what you actually plan to take – this may vary depending on race conditions. Make sure that all the clothing you plan to take is included – for example, if you're doing a cold-weather race, you'll need extra layers and jacket.
- Get out your kitchen scales and weigh every piece of equipment

This equipment list was originally developed for a 4 Deserts race and has been refined to suit several subsequent self-supported 5 or 6 stage races. (Self-supported refers to stage races where you have to carry your food and equipment with you at all times).

Tips:

- Get out your kitchen scales and weigh every piece of equipment you plan to take, then update the weights on the tracker (you can use the weights left in there, but beware: they might not be accurate for your gear)

- Come up with a nutrition plan for the week and input every piece of food you intend to take with you. I've included a summary which calculates how much your pack will weigh after each day (subtracting the food you are eating) which is a nice indicator, and also included space for calories, and a quick calorie / gram calculator for your reference.

Note: **a downloadable, Excel-based version** of the below list is available over at MarathonHandbook.com right now - just go to the Stage Race section. It includes rough weights for each item and automatically calculates your total pack weight, your pack weight after each day (minus the food you eat) and the calories you eat.

Item Description	Weight (g)	Packed?
In The Backpack		
Backpack		
Sleeping bag		
headlamp		
headlamp (back-up)		
Flashing LED Safety Light		
multi-tool (knife)		
Safety Whistle		
Mirror		
Emergency Bivvy		
Compass		
Spork		
Sunblock		
lip balm (+ SPF)		
Medication - Paracetamol and Imodium		
Blister Kit		

Cotton Crepe Bandage		
safety pins		
Alcohol Gel		
tablet towels and wet wipes		
2 spare pairs of socks		
long shorts (compression)		
shirt for camp		
waterproof Jacket		
warm long sleeved top		
2 water bottles		
inflatable sleeping pad		
Buff		
flip-flops		
toothbrush and toothpaste		
Ipod shuffle with headphones		
Bodyglide anti-chafe		
KT tape		
earplugs		
Camera		
paper and pen		

platypus (collapsible water bottle)		
shampoo sachets		
zip lock bags		
total non-food items weight:		
Clothing (worn during race)		
shoes		
shorts		
Long sleeved shirt		
hat		
sunglasses		
socks		
watch		
total clothing worn during race weight:		g
Food		
Item Description	Weight (g)	cal
Tea Bags		

Instant Coffee (10 sachets)		
total		
Pre-Race (evening only required)		
1 x dehydrated meal		
daily total		
Stage 1		
2 x noodles		
5 x gels		
1 x dehydrated meal		
daily total		
Stage 2		
1 x dehydrated breakfast		
2 x gels		
2x clif bars		
sports beans		
50g beef jerky		
50g nuts		

1 x dehydrated meal		
Protein shake		
daily total		
Stage 3		
1 x dehydrated breakfast		
2 x gels		
2x clif bars		
sports beans		
50g beef jerky		
50g nuts		
1 x dehydrated meal		
Protein shake		
daily total		
Stage 4		
1 x dehydrated breakfast		
2 x gels		
2x clif bars		
sports beans		

50g beef jerky		
50g nuts		
1 x dehydrated meal		
Protein shake		
daily total		
Stage 5		
1 x dehydrated breakfast		
6 x gels		
3x clif bars		
sports beans		
2 x 50g beef jerky		
2 x 50g nuts		
1 x dehydrated meal		
Protein shake		
daily total		
Rest Day		
1 x dehydrated breakfast		
1 x clif bar		

1 x dehydrated meal		
daily total		
Stage 6 (10km)		
1 x dehydrated breakfast		
daily total		
FOOD TOTAL	g	cal
BACKPACK TOTAL (At Start of Race)	g	

APPENDIX - EXAMPLE EQUIPMENT LIST: SUPPORTED STAGE RACE

The below equipment and food list includes all the typical equipment a runner might take to a supported stage race, where their pack is transported from camp to camp - it is not race-specific and not necessarily comprehensive. See the Equipment and Race Preparation chapters for much more on this.

Supported races differ from self-supported races in that your daily gear bag is transported from camp to camp, meaning you only need to carry with you a small pack for daily food, maybe a waterproof layer, and any essentials that the race director insists on. As there is minimal carrying required, I haven't included an input section for the weight of each piece of gear in the spreadsheet.

I've used this equipment list on several Global Limits races and the Burgos Way of Legends race, and it has now been used by many other runners for their supported stage race.

How to Use:

- Download the Equipment List below over at marathonhandbook.com in the Stage Race section.
- Check it first against your race's mandatory and optional equipment lists, to make sure it covers everything the race director has told you to take.

- Check it against what you actually plan to take – this may vary depending on race conditions. Make sure that all the clothing you plan to take is included – for example, if you're doing a cold-weather race, you'll need extra layers and jacket.
- Get out your kitchen scales and weigh every piece of equipment

Note: **a downloadable, Excel-based version** of the below list is available over at MarathonHandbook.com right now - just go to the Stage Race section. It includes rough weights for each item and automatically calculates your total pack weight, your pack weight after each day (minus the food you eat) and the calories you eat.

THE STAGE RACE HANDBOOK

Item Description	Packed?	Notes
Camp Items (ex. Food)		
Big backpack (camp bag)		
sleeping bag		
Flashing LED Safety Light		
Survival Blanket		
Spork		
Lip balm and sun block, 0.15oz		
Medication - Paracetamol and Imodium		
Blister Kit		
8 safety pins		
tablet towels and wet wipes		
3 pairs of socks		
trousers for camp		
havianas		
toothbrush and toothpaste		
anti-chafe		
Kinseo tape		
earplugs		

iPhone		
paper and cheap pen		
zip lock bags		
Camp clothes		
Running Equipment (for race backpack)		
Running backpack (lightweight - 8l)		
Running Clothing		
Running Shoes		
Running shorts		
Running shirt		
hat		
sunglasses		
watch		
Running Socks		
LED Headlamp + spare batts		
Multi-tool		
Safety Whistle		
Alcohol Gel		
waterproof Jacket		

Buff		
Ipod shuffles with headphones		
Food Items		
Tea Bags		
Instant Coffee (10 sachets)		
Salt tablets for the week		
First Night		
1 x dehydrated meal		
Stage 1		
1 noodles breakfast		
3 x gels		
150gram of jerky / crisps / nut mix		
1 x dehydrated meal		
Stage 2		
1 noodles breakfast		
3 x gels		

150gram of jerky / crisps / nut mix		
1 x dehydrated meal		
Stage 3		
1 noodles breakfast		
3 x gels		
225gram of jerky / crisps / nut mix		
1 x dehydrated meal		
Stage 4		
1 noodles breakfast		
4 x gels		
300gram of jerky / crisps / nut mix		
1 x dehydrated meal		
Stage 5		
1 noodles breakfast		
3 x gels		
150gram of jerky / crisps / nut mix		
1 x dehydrated meal		

Stage 6		
1 noodles breakfast		
1 gel		

Printed in Great Britain
by Amazon